Religious School of the
WILSHIRE BOULEVARD TEMPLE

This Book Belongs to

Barbara Loeb

Grade [redacted] 7 Room [redacted] Saturday ☒ Sunday ☐ Monday ☐

1962/63-5723

THE *New* JEWISH HISTORY

BOOK TWO

From the Maccabees to the
Discovery of America

THE PUBLICATION of this volume
The New Jewish History
was made possible by the estab-
lishment of a fund for the
publication of Jewish religious
school literature by the
NATIONAL FEDERATION OF TEMPLE SISTERHOODS

BOOK TWO

THE *New* JEWISH HISTORY

From the Maccabees to the Discovery of America

MAMIE G. GAMORAN

Illustrated by BRUNO FROST

THE *Union*
OF AMERICAN HEBREW CONGREGATIONS
New York, N. Y.

NEW YORK, N. Y.

Third Printing, 1960

PRINTED IN U. S. OF AMERICA

TO MY
GRANDNEPHEWS AND GRANDNIECE
ALAN, PETER, BILLY B. AND BILLY S., AMY,
AND JONATHAN

EDITOR'S INTRODUCTION

The aim of *The New Jewish History* by Mamie G. Gamoran is, as we explained in the introduction to Book One, chiefly threefold: to emphasize what is interesting and dramatic in the story of the Jewish people; to stress the achievements of Judaism, particularly in the areas of social, religious, and cultural values; and, in telling the story of Jewish persecution, which cannot be ignored, to accent the inner fortitude which made it possible for Jews and Judaism to survive, holding aloft our great Jewish ideals despite tragedy.

Book Two tells, among other things, the story of Jewish persecution and of the years of the Crusades. These events were treated with particular care in order to emphasize the courage of a people steadfast in their adherence to their traditions and values at a time of adversity.

Above all, the author sought to keep in mind the desirability of creating positive attitudes on the part of our children. They are to be led to feel that the history of their people is an unfinished story in which they will participate; that it is dramatic and challenging; and that the Jewish people have made important contributions to the world and to the peoples in whose midst they lived. It is a record of continuous achievement in spite of many adverse circumstances. The account is therefore given as a running story, to hold the interest of the child. The events are presented for their dramatic quality and for their record of significant Jewish achievement along cultural, ethical, and spiritual lines. To what extent the author has succeeded in fulfilling these aims, our readers will have to judge.

Teachers have often expressed the thought that little children can learn in school only through the story-telling, dramatizing method. When they grow older, they are ready to receive information, and when they grow still older and are in high school, they begin to reason. Hence, writers of textbooks for younger children have felt that they must take only emotional appeals into consideration. This division has long been abandoned. We now know that children feel, learn, and think at the same time. To be sure, the writer has to bear in mind the age group for which he is writing, but youngsters often surprise us by their thinking ability. It is not wise to underrate them.

Bearing the above thoughts in mind, the author has sought to present the facts of Jewish history frankly; to teach children that the characters on the stage of our history are not perfect, that they have their human weaknesses, and that it is our duty to present a truthful account in accordance with our best knowledge of what transpired.

Book Two, which begins with the Maccabean victory and ends with the discovery of America, includes the end of the Second Commonwealth, the rise of Christianity, the development of the Talmud—Mishnah and Gemara—the Crusades, and the expulsion from Spain. It constitutes a special challenge to any author who seeks to emphasize the positive approach to Jewish life. It is hoped that teachers and supervisors will write us and give us their suggestions and criticisms, bearing in mind our criteria, and tell us to what extent the book succeeds in conveying to our pupils the story of Jewish achievements over the years and a sense of the inner fortitude which characterized our people during the difficult periods of persecution.

An Activity Book has been issued to accompany this text. It is hoped that teachers in particular will give us their concrete suggestions on this phase of the work.

Emanuel Gamoran

ACKNOWLEDGMENTS

It is a pleasant task to acknowledge my gratitude to those who helped in the preparation of Book Two of *The New Jewish History*.

My first thanks go to the reading committee of the Commission on Jewish Education, composed of Dr. Leon Fram, Chairman, Dr. Solomon B. Freehof, and Dr. Harry M. Orlinsky, who went over the manuscript with great care and gave me the benefit of their wide knowledge of history and of their educational experience.

Mr. Samuel Grand and Rabbi Eugene Lipman read the manuscript and made a number of helpful, critical suggestions. Miss Mimi Levy of the Little Red Schoolhouse in New York City was of assistance because of her teaching experience on the level for which the book is intended. Her comments on questions of child-interest and word comprehension were especially valuable.

The format of the book, a companion to Book One, is most pleasing. For this credit must be given to Mr. Ralph Davis. Mrs. Julia Minor and Miss Sylvia Schiff helped in the many details which transform a typewritten manuscript into a book. I am grateful to all of them.

The translations of the poems of Solomon ibn Gabirol and Yehuda Halevi used in Chapter 23 are simplified versions of those found in *Selected Religious Poems of Solomon ibn Gabirol* translated by Israel Zangwill, and *Selected Poems of Jehudah Halevi* translated by Nina Salaman, both published by the Jewish Publication Society. I am pleased to call attention to these excellent books.

Acknowledgments are due to Farrar, Straus and Cudahy, Inc.

for permission to use excerpts from *A Treasury of Hebrew Letters* by Franz Kobler, in Chapter 24.

The editor, as always, was guide and critic. I tried to follow the basic ideas which he laid down for this history—the drama, achievements, and spiritual values inherent in the story of the Jewish people.

In the final analysis, it is the children who use the books who decide whether I have succeeded. They have been generous in their response to Book One; it is my earnest hope that Book Two will meet their exacting judgment.

M. G. G.

New York, September, 1956

CONTENTS

THE *New* JEWISH HISTORY

BOOK TWO

From the Maccabees to the
Discovery of America

Read This Before You Begin the Book

You are now ready to go on with your study of Jewish history. I wonder how you will answer these questions. Were you pleased with what you learned about your early ancestors? Did you enjoy sharing the experiences of the men and women of Israel and Judah? Did the story of how the Bible came into being, and what it means to the world today, impress you? Did the words of the prophets ring in your ears? And did you breathe a sigh of relief when you learned that the people of Judea were to be at peace under a ruler of their own choosing?

I hope you also have a feeling of curiosity. You ask, what happens next? Book Two of *The New Jewish History* was written to answer your question.

Your new book covers more than 1,500 years of Jewish history. You leave the little land of Palestine to travel to other parts of Asia, to Europe and Africa. You even touch the fringes of the new world, America.

New names, far-away places, strange and exciting experiences, are in store for you. Another great literary work, the Talmud, is completed. Together, the Bible and the Talmud become pillars of strength in days of trouble. The ideals of our early teachers are not forgotten. They influence men and women who live in other lands and other days. Wonderful periods of freedom where wise thinkers write and teach, and splendid poets sing, are just ahead.

The story of your people is a breath-taking tale. It should hold you, it should teach you. You will want to have a share in it.

And now let us go on.

Unit 1

Maccabean Freedom and Roman Rule

Book I closed with the splendid story of the Maccabean victory. We begin our story now with the years of independence under Maccabean rule.

The Jews were faced with a choice. They could develop into a nation like other nations, ambitious for land and power. They might, however, try to create a people living modestly on their own land, finding a way of life based on ancient traditions which had served them well.

Two parties developed with different points of view on the future of the nation, the life of its people, and the Bible, the law of the land.

The people were divided. Whom should they follow? Could they find a way which spelled progress and also allowed them to continue in the path which Judaism had set out for them? Would a powerful nation which came to rule over them influence their choice?

Hail Simon, the Maccabee!

1. THE FIRST YEARS

INDEPENDENCE! The Syrian soldiers finally left the land. Joy and relief filled the hearts of the Jews. Simon, the Maccabee, had been chosen High Priest and Prince. He was a fine person to lead the country at this time. He traveled about from town to village to see for himself how best he could help his people. After the years of war and trouble, his steady hand and wise mind guided the nation well.

A pact of friendship was made with Syria. All debts which Judea had owed Syria through taxes and tribute were canceled. Syria agreed that Judea would not have to pay any tribute in the future. Simon took over two fortresses which strengthened Judea's military position. One fortress commanded the mountain passes which led to the seaport of Joppa, and the other was a citadel of Jerusalem.

Although Simon was greatly beloved, the Great Assembly which chose him to be their ruler did not give him the title of King. They declared that Simon and his descendants should rule until "a true prophet shall arise from Israel." By this they meant until a member of the house of King David could be placed upon the throne.

During the seven years of Simon's rule, Judea had a taste of what peace and freedom could mean. How different life

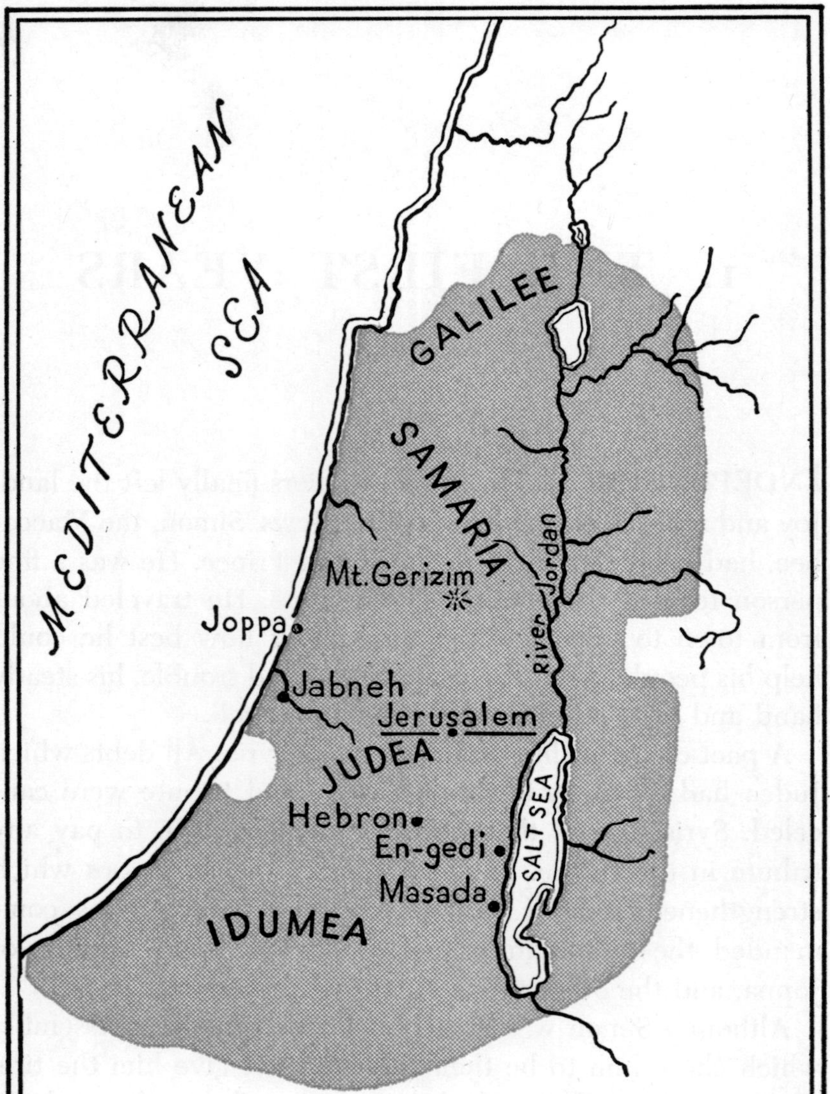

Palestine in the Days of the Maccabean Kings

was when men did not have to leave their homes to fight! Farmers reclaimed their lands. Craftsmen went back to their tools and their benches. Scribes and teachers taught in schools and academies. The nation could prosper during years of peace.

The writer of the First Book of Maccabees, which tells of the exploits of all the Maccabees, described Simon's rule in a way which showed the admiration and love which the people had for their leader. He said, "Then did the people till their ground in peace, and the earth gave her increase, and the trees of the field their fruit. He (Simon) provided victuals for the cities, and made peace in the land, and Israel rejoiced with great joy. For every man sat under his vine and his figtree, and there was none to fight against them. He strengthened all those of his people who were brought low. Every wicked person he took away. He beautified the sanctuary, and multiplied the vessels of the Temple."

Simon wanted to make Judea safe. A little country like his could never stand alone. It had to have friends. The new and powerful empire of Rome was beginning to show its

strength. It had sent conquering armies as far north as what is now France, and up to the British Isles. Nearer home, it was the master of Egypt, of Greece, and of Syria. Simon sent a delegation to the emperor at Rome. As was usually the case on a mission of friendship, they carried with them a beautiful gift. It was a heavy golden shield which was received with great thanks.

Good news came to Jerusalem. The messengers returned with a treaty of peace which declared that Rome recognized Judea as an independent state and hoped the two countries would be friendly to each other. The consul at Rome wrote letters to the heads of many neighboring countries telling of the treaty he had just made, and asking them also to be friendly with Judea.

Simon's son, John Hyrcanus, had great ambitions. When he became ruler, he determined to widen the boundaries of his land. His mind went back to earlier days, to a larger kingdom. He hired soldiers and sent them north and south, where they fought and conquered. He overcame the Samaritans, living on Mt. Gerizim. Only a few families escaped from his soldiers. Their descendants, few in number, live today in Shechem in the Kingdom of Jordan, although some of them came over the border to live in Jerusalem, in Israel. To the south, Edom, that old enemy, was conquered.

John Hyrcanus had another idea. Not only would his territory grow, but he would find more followers for his religion. He ordered the people who lived in the conquered areas to become Jews! The Idumeans, as the Edomites were called, were forced to accept Judaism as their religion. What a strange action for a son of the Maccabees, who gave their lives for religious freedom! In this way, the Idumeans became subjects of Judea and forced converts to the Jewish religion.

Simon's descendants were not satisfied with the proclamation of forty years earlier. His grandson, Alexander, declared himself king. He ruled for almost thirty years. He and his advisers wanted a bigger country, and they succeeded in their ambitions. More and more territory was added. Judea extended almost as far as Judah had in the days of Solomon. The country was prosperous and wealthy.

In spite of these flourishing conditions, all was not well in the land. Some people had not been pleased when the Idumeans were forced to become Jews. They were eager to have more men and women follow Judaism, but not through force—only because they honestly believed in the ideals of the prophets and of the Bible.

These men realized that the Jewish people could not count their victories in the same way as other nations. Size and power were not the measuring rods of their history. They knew many examples to show this. While the Hebrew slaves were but a disorganized group, their leader gave them and the world the Ten Commandments. The messages of the prophets were delivered while Israel and Judah were small countries. The Bible came into being during the years that Judea was a tiny forgotten fragment in the Persian Empire. Surely independence must mean more to the Jewish people than conquest and the subjection of other peoples to their will and rule.

The people were divided on many serious questions. A sharp line separated a number of groups in the country from each other. The two largest parties disagreed about how their country should be governed and about its future. These differences were both political and religious. The names of these two groups are the Sadducees and the Pharisees. To understand what happened in the years that followed the rule of

John Hyrcanus and King Alexander, we must know more about these parties.

SOMETHING TO TALK OVER IN CLASS

Why would Judah Maccabee have objected to the action of John Hyrcanus?

What is the difference between:

A law which says children must go to school between the ages of six and sixteen?

A law which says every man must change his religion to the religion of the conqueror?

SOMETHING TO DO

Make a list of the benefits which came to the people of Judea under Simon's rule.

READ

The Unconquered by Joseph Gaer, "King David's Treasure," p. 207.

Great Men in Israel by J. Max Weis, "The King and the Judge," p. 10.

SOMETHING IMPORTANT TO KNOW

Sometimes we use the words "The Second Commonwealth." The period which the Second Commonwealth covers began with the year 586 B.C.E. and continued up to the year 70 C.E.

READINGS FOR TEACHERS

Unit 1 (*CHAPTERS 1–5*)

A History of the Jews by Solomon Grayzel, Chap. V, pp. 71–120; Chap. VI, pp. 121–136.

A History of the Jewish People by Max L. Margolis and Alexander Marx, Chaps. XXVII, XXVIII, and XXIX.

The Jewish Festivals by Hayyim Schauss, Chap. XV, pp. 125–142.

Hillel by Ely M. Pilchik.

2. PARTIES IN PALESTINE

THE PARTIES of the Sadducees and the Pharisees did not grow up over night. Their ways of thinking and living took long years to develop. The Sadducees came into existence in the years which followed the return from Babylonia, during the period of the theocracy, when the High Priest was both the political and the religious ruler. It is possible that the name Sadducees comes from the name of Zadok, the priest appointed by King Solomon to lead the Temple services in his day. The High Priest was usually a Sadducee, and most of the time he was the head of the Sanhedrin, the highest court of the land. If not he, another high-ranking Sadducee was generally chosen for this important post. The wealthy merchants, the officers of the army, and the influential priests were Sadducees. Rich landowners and merchants were not pleased when Simon was selected to become High Priest and Prince of the land, since he came from a family of lower-ranking priests, but Simon was so popular that the people swept him into his high office.

The name of the second large group of people is also very interesting. To this day, we are not sure of its exact meaning. The Pharisees, or in Hebrew, the P'rushim, could mean those who separated themselves (perhaps from the Sadducees), or "those who explained." The second meaning may be the real one, for the rabbis, the teachers, and the scribes were found among the Pharisees.

Although the Sadducees were smaller in number than the Pharisees, they had been the ruling group for many years. Most of the kings who followed John Hyrcanus looked to the Sadducees for guidance.

History has taught us that ruling groups are very slow to change. They like things as they are. Politically, the Sadducees wanted to continue to be the governing group. They encouraged the king in his desire to enlarge the nation. Religiously, they were opposed to any changes. The Sadducees believed that the Jews should pattern their life on the laws of the Torah as they had been written down years before. They were firm on this point. They did not wish any changes to be made either in the laws of sacrifice, Temple worship, or daily living.

The Pharisees were closer to the masses of the people, more democratic and more interested in the every-day life of the men and women of the country. Their attitude toward the Temple sacrifices shows this clearly. To buy the animals and birds which were used for the sacrifices cost a great deal of money. While the Sadducees were the leading group, only wealthy families made the large contributions which paid for the sacrifices. When the Pharisees gained influence, a new law was passed which gave every man a share in the Temple sacrifices. Each Jew paid at least one-half shekel to the Temple treasury. His contribution was both a duty and a privilege. The poor as well as the rich shared in the Temple service and in the sacrifices.

Another way of sharing was begun by the Pharisees. They divided the country into twenty-four sections. Some men from each section went to the Temple and attended the sacrifices.

Since not every man could go, those who stayed at home gathered together to read portions of the Torah. The Pharisees fostered a feeling of unity among all the people which the Sadducees had not tried to bring about.

But the most important difference between Pharisees and Sadducees came from their attitude on the laws of the Bible. The Pharisees agreed with the Sadducees that the Torah must be the law of the land. Everyone believed this. Since the time of Ezra, the people of Judea had been governed by the laws of the Bible. Marriage was regulated by Biblical law. Debts and property were managed by the laws of the Torah.

As times changed, the Pharisees believed that the laws had to change, too. Unless they were explained or changed when necessary, they would not work properly for the good of the people.

In the course of hundreds of years, there will be changes in the way any people live. In the eleven or twelve years of your life, and certainly in the lifetime of your parents, there have been many changes. The new and wonderful knowledge of the atom and its powers was learned only a few years ago. The first plane to gain national fame rose in the air in 1903. Perhaps you have been in an airplane more than once. When your father was a boy he probably did not take a trip by plane. He certainly could not turn on a television set when he was eleven years old; there just wasn't one in existence. Laws have had to be created to govern these new marvels of our time.

Important matters which have to do with the welfare of our country have changed too. In the early years of this century, thousands of immigrants came to America every month. Anyone who wished to enter was permitted to come in, if he was healthy and had a small sum of money to start him on his own. At present, immigration is strictly limited for many reasons. Here is another example. There are cities where men could not get jobs because of their race, their color, or their religion. This is impossible now in many states. Such changes come about through new laws or through changes in old laws. That is why our Senators and Congressmen are called lawmakers.

Two thousand years ago, life did not move as swiftly as it does in America today. Changes were more gradual. But changes there were. Judea became a fairly large and busy country instead of a small, quiet, agricultural land. Landowners with good-sized farms employed many workers, or rented out the land to men whose families tilled the soil.

Farm products went to the cities at home and to other nations as well. Rich crops of wheat and barley, and grapes of unusual quality found ready markets outside of Judea. Its terraced hills held large groves of olive trees. The tiny green

fruit of these trees yielded food and oil. Oil was one of the products used by everybody, everywhere. Oil filled lamps at night, softened the skin after days of dusty travel, and was used in every home for cooking. It was sold in great quantities.

The names, Judea and Jerusalem, were known in all the countries around the Mediterranean Sea. Jewish merchants had connections with traders in many countries. Judean ships sailed to other ports. Jewish pilgrims came from foreign lands to celebrate the festivals in Jerusalem. Many outward changes in the size, position, and ways of life in Palestine had occurred.

Explanations and additions to fit new conditions had been given to the laws of the Torah by learned scribes and rabbis for many years. These were not written down. They had been stated by the rabbi and repeated by his pupils. These explanations were called the Oral Law, while the Bible was called the Written Law. Oral comes from a Latin word which means "uttered by the mouth," that is, "spoken." You use this word at school when you say "oral arithmetic." You know the difference between oral arithmetic and written arithmetic. The Pharisees accepted the Oral Law while the Sadducees usually followed the Written Law.

An example of how the Oral Law influenced the life of the people will help you to understand the difference between the Pharisees and the Sadducees. The Bible says, "An eye for an eye, and a tooth for a tooth." That is, if a person loses an eye through another man's fault, the second man must be punished by losing an eye. The Oral Law declared that this did not mean actually giving up an eye; the offender could pay his victim money for the loss of the eye. This explanation was followed by the Pharisees; the Sadducees were ready to carry out the law as it was written in the Bible.

The ruling on debts and the Sabbatical year which was made by the great teacher, Hillel, also shows how the Pharisees adapted an old law to new conditions.

According to the Torah, every seventh year was a Sabbatical year. No taxes were collected during such a year. Debts were canceled. In this way, a poor man had a chance to make a fresh start without debts hanging over him. A rich man had to be satisfied to lose some money for the sake of his poorer brethren. During the years when Judea was an agricultural community, the law was useful and was followed. Debts were probably small and might have been repaid in work or in produce. When commerce and industry were introduced into the country, large sums of money were involved. As the seventh year approached, people could not borrow money. Lenders hesitated to lend. They thought they would lose their money. This was hard on men who were ready to repay loans even during the Sabbatical year. Business suffered.

Hillel found a solution which became part of the Oral Law. The loans were made through the Sanhedrin, which in turn collected the debt. No individual borrowed or lent. No one had to feel that he was violating the Torah.

The Oral Law did not take the place of the Written Law. It was an addition or an explanation. The Oral Law helped to keep Judaism alive. To make progress means sometimes to change. The Pharisees believed in a living Judaism which would help men to live good and honorable lives and come closer to God. They did not want their religion to become dry and formal and fixed in the ways of by-gone days.

The Pharisees and the Sadducees were not the only groups in Palestine. One small group of men broke away from the Pharisees and formed a division called Essenes. The Essenes observed very strictly all the rules and regulations of daily living found in the Torah. They kept the rules of the Sabbath very carefully. In order to do this they lived apart in small groups in villages of their own, for they could not live as they wished in towns and cities with other people. In these villages of the Essenes, no man owned anything for himself; everything belonged to the community. They ate only vegetarian food, wore plain white linen clothes, and became skilled in treating sick people with simple herbs and plants. They washed themselves frequently, to be clean and pure. Most of the Essenes lived at En-gedi near the Dead Sea desert. Because of their ideas of purity, strict religious beliefs, and simple ways of living, the Essenes were respected by their fellow Jews.

In the past few years, in the area of the Dead Sea, a number of ancient Hebrew scrolls were found by wandering Bedouins. Many scholars believe that these scrolls were the possession of the Essenes or some other Jewish group who hid them in jars in time of trouble, perhaps when Roman soldiers were in the vicinity. As these scrolls are being deciphered by scholars, we are learning much more about sects like the Essenes and about the life of their times.

The differences in the ideas of the Sadducees and the Pharisees had an important influence on the happenings of the years that followed.

SOMETHING TO DO

Make three headings as follows:

SADDUCEES PHARISEES ESSENES

Under each heading write some of the ideas of each group.

SOMETHING TO THINK ABOUT

A. What are three ways in which our country has changed since it was discovered?

Name three inventions or discoveries which have been made since the early days of America. Did laws have to be passed to take care of the changes in our country, and of new inventions or discoveries?

B. How did the Pharisees give all the people a share in Temple worship?

READ

Hillel by Pilchik, "The More Counsel the More Understanding," p. 67.

3. DEFEAT IN VICTORY

A SADDUCEE ruler and a Pharisee people could not get along. One believed in conquest and armies to win new territory for him. The other wanted the opportunity to live in peace, and to erect schools and synagogues for education and worship.

The rivalry between the Sadducees and the Pharisees was bitter. King Alexander treated the Pharisees badly. He believed they were his enemies. He did not consult them nor give them high places in the government. For some unknown reason, he changed his mind before he died. He named his wife, Queen Salome, to reign after him. He advised her to call in the Pharisees to help her rule the country when she became queen.

Queen Salome reigned for nine years, wisely and well. She followed Alexander's advice. During her reign the Pharisees came to power. Her chief adviser was a learned rabbi named Simon ben Shetach. He was appointed President of the Sanhedrin.

The Talmud says, "Under Simon ben Shetach and Queen Salome, rain fell on the eve of the Sabbath, so that the corns of wheat were as large as kidneys, and the barley corns as large as olives." Of course, neither the queen nor her adviser were rainmakers, but they were given credit for the good

weather because they brought peace and plenty to the land.

The Pharisees did not use their power to fight wars or to conquer more territory. They used it to better the life of the people. They opened schools all over the country, in the large villages, towns, and cities. They reminded judges to be fair and impartial at trials. The judges were told to examine a witness at a trial very carefully, to make sure he did not contradict himself at any time, and to guard against falsehoods which might hurt a man on trial.

The good years of Queen Salome's reign might have continued. When Salome died her two sons came to a peaceful agreement. Hyrcanus, the older, would continue to serve as High Priest, as he had during Salome's reign. Aristobulus, the younger, would become king. Such an arrangement was pleasing to the Pharisees, who did not like to see the High Priest act as king. They believed that the High Priest should be a man whose life was given over completely to religious work and to the service of the Temple. A king had affairs of state to carry on which could take him away from his religious duties.

But the agreement did not stand, and civil war broke out. For almost five years the rival brothers fought against each other. Neither side was winning. The two groups looked for an outsider to decide their fate. Pompey, a famous Roman general, was resting in Syria after great victories. Both brothers sent delegations to Pompey with rich gifts and begged him to decide who should be king.

Another group came to Pompey—a delegation representing the people. They had a different request. They wanted Palestine to be ruled once again by a High Priest, as it had been in the quiet years after Ezra's time. They were tired of kings and of warfare.

Pompey decided. He chose Hyrcanus. Aristobulus was too strong, too independent, to suit Rome. Pompey enforced his decree by a fierce attack upon the forces of Aristobulus in Jerusalem. He finally won by storming Jerusalem on the Sabbath.

Hyrcanus' victory was also a defeat. He did not become king. He was named Ethnarch, ruler under Rome. Nor did he rule alone. His adviser was Antipater, an Idumean, who had become a Jew when his country was conquered by John Hyrcanus, years before. Antipater, the Idumean, had urged Hyrcanus to fight against his brother. Now he guided every move which Hyrcanus made.

Antipater's two sons were placed in positions of importance. One was appointed governor of the district of Jerusalem, and one was the governor of Galilee. The forced conversion of the Idumeans was to have an unhappy influence on the Jewish people.

The period of independence lasted for about eighty years, from 142 B.C.E. to 63 B.C.E. Now it came to an end. From now on, Judea was a province of Rome. Jewish rulers sat on the throne. The High Priest served in the Temple. But both were chosen by Rome. Rome had added one more country to the long list of nations which made up her vast empire.

SOMETHING TO TALK OVER IN CLASS

Was it good to separate the offices of High Priest and king? Why?

Are religious affairs and state affairs separate in our country?

READ

The Unconquered by Gaer, "There Was Once a Queen," p. 238; "Pompey's Discovery," p. 267.

4. A CRUEL MONARCH

THE SANHEDRIN in Jerusalem was the highest court of the land. It was called the Great Sanhedrin. It had seventy members, plus the president, drawn from the most important men in the country. These men would rule on all questions of religious law. Sometimes they had to examine a law in the Torah which did not seem to be clear, and explain what it meant to the people of that day. Sometimes they acted as a court of justice and tried criminals who came before them. All their rulings were based on the laws in the Bible. Therefore, the members of the Sanhedrin had to be scholars and learned men. One writer says that the Sanhedrin drew its members from a "well of justice, mercy, and wisdom."

In order for their judgments to be respected, they also had to be men whom the people thought well of, because of their family connections and their place in the community. Sometimes the leaders of the Sanhedrin were Sadducees. Then the laws were followed strictly, as they were found in the Bible. Sometimes the most important members of the Sanhedrin were Pharisees. They would use the Oral Law to help them act wisely and justly.

There were other, smaller courts, also called Sanhedrins. These had twenty-three members. Sanhedrins of this size were found in Jerusalem and in other cities as well. They dealt with minor questions of law and with personal and civil offenses. The smaller Sanhedrins were supervised by the Great Sanhedrin, which was the supreme religious authority. No Sanhedrin had the power to act in political cases. Crimes against the state had to be brought before Roman authorities.

When a man was called before the Great Sanhedrin, he came humbly dressed in dark clothes, awaiting the just decision of the court.

One man defied the Sanhedrin when he was summoned to appear before it. He strode in, dressed in fine robes, carrying weapons, and with him came a bodyguard of soldiers.

The rabbis and leaders who were members of the Sanhedrin were astonished. King Hyrcanus, the president, said

nothing to the man who so impudently entered the council chamber, for it was Herod, son of Antipater, and friend of Rome. Hyrcanus did not disclose the fact that he had received a letter from the emperor saying that no harm must come to Herod.

The charge was read. Herod was then the governor of Galilee, the northern part of Palestine. In Galilee hatred of Rome ran high. Herod was accused of ordering the killing of Hezekiah, a Jewish warrior, and many of his followers. These men had tried to lead a rebellion against Rome. Herod had condemned Hezekiah without a fair trial. The charge was not denied. Herod was guilty.

Some of the judges of the Sanhedrin feared Herod's power. But one judge, named Shemayah, spoke up with great courage. He said, "Never before has anyone come before us, proud and haughty, dressed in purple, with armed men about him. And you, for the sake of the king, are ready to dismiss him. I say that if you do so, this man will some day punish you and your king."

Shemayah's words were heard by the Sanhedrin. Judgment against Herod was about to be passed. Hyrcanus had to do something. He reminded the judges of a ruling which said that a man could not be convicted on the same day he was charged with his crime. He dismissed the court. Herod fled from Jerusalem that night. The brave words of Shemayah had no results.

Only a few years later, this same Herod, who once stood before the Sanhedrin, was appointed by the Roman emperor to the throne.

In those few years, Hyrcanus had lost his throne and his office of High Priest through a rebellion led by his nephew. In turn, Herod displaced the new king who reigned for only two years. Instead of a Maccabee, an Idumean sat on the throne of Judea.

For forty-one years Herod ruled. He was a cruel and wicked monarch, hated by his subjects. One of his first acts was to order the execution of a number of wealthy Jews, whose possessions he then took for himself. Among them were members of the same Sanhedrin which had tried him. Shemayah's words came true.

Herod did not feel secure on the throne of Palestine. He knew that the people were still loyal to the Maccabean family. Mariamne, his beautiful wife, was a granddaughter of Hyrcanus and a direct descendant of Simon the Maccabee. Herod may have thought that for her sake the people would rally to him. He saw, however, that the queen's brother, who was the rightful heir to the throne, was very popular. When he went through the streets of Jerusalem, he was received with shouts of joy. This young man lost his life in a strange accident while swimming. Other members of the royal court, including Hyrcanus, were done away with, one by one. At last, in a fit of anger, Mariamne was put to death at Herod's command. Through these wicked acts, the king lost any loyalty he might have won.

Because Herod pleased the Roman emperors, he received gifts of cities from them. Some of these were places which had been taken away from earlier Jewish rulers after Rome took control of the country. Some of these cities were inhabited by Greeks and other non-Jews. Palestine therefore had large areas which were wholly non-Jewish. This was one of the reasons why the Pharisees insisted so on Jewish observances and ceremonials, and on Jewish learning. On many sides, Greek, Roman, and other non-Jewish influences could easily have crept into Jewish life, unless sharp eyes kept watch and strong efforts were made to keep them out.

A few such cities, with Greek names and Greek and Roman inhabitants, formed a league called the Decapolis. (Decapolis means "ten cities," but sometimes there were twelve or even fourteen cities in the league.) At times some of them were

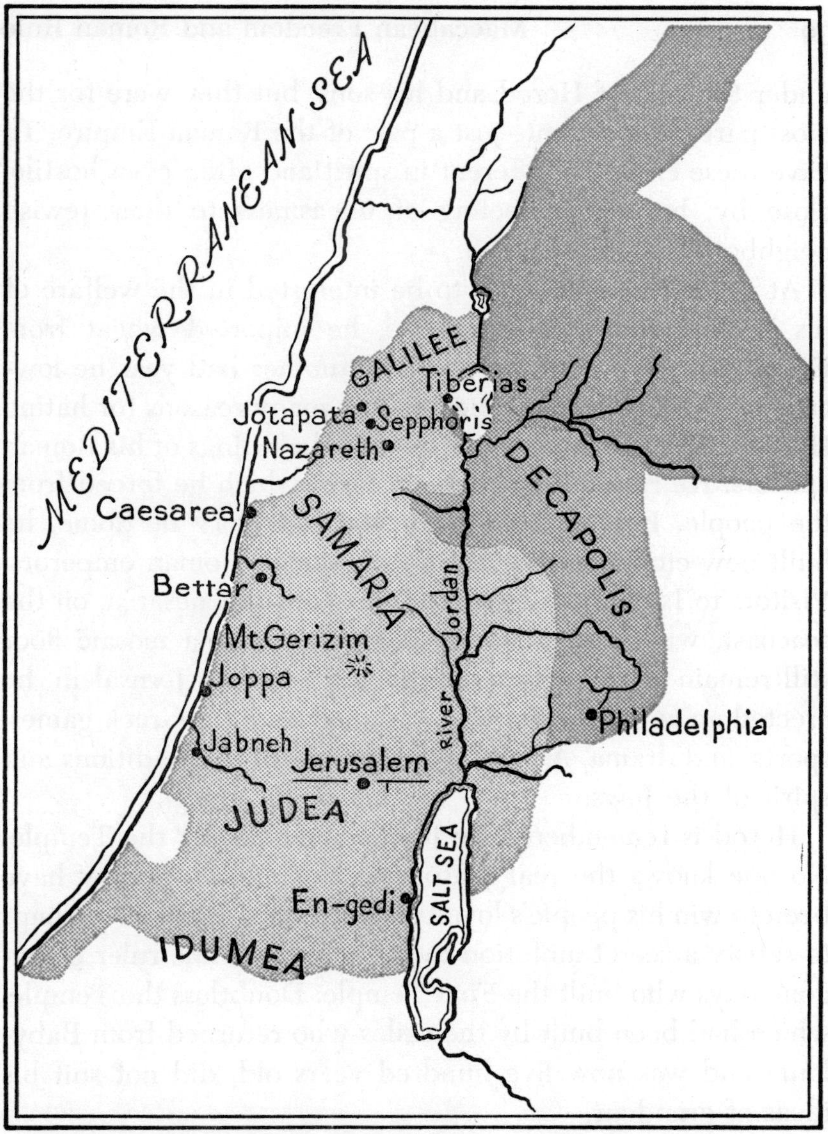

Palestine in the Days of the Romans

under the rule of Herod and his sons, but they were for the most part independent—just a part of the Roman Empire. To have these cities, so different in spirit and often even hostile, close by, brought a feeling of uneasiness to their Jewish neighbors.

At times Herod seemed to be interested in the welfare of his people. In years of famine, he imported wheat from Egypt and gave it to the poor. In another bad year he lowered taxes. However, the people had many reasons for hating Herod. He was ready always to obey the rulings of his Roman masters. He raised huge sums in taxes which he forced from the people. For his own glory and the glory of Rome, he built new cities, naming them in honor of Roman emperors. Visitors to Israel today may see the ruins of Caesarea, on the seacoast, where huge stones and pillars and a mosaic floor still remain of this city which Herod built. In Jerusalem, he erected an amphitheater and a hippodrome for Greek games, sports, and drama. All this was contrary to the traditions and spirit of the Jews.

Herod is remembered by Jews for rebuilding the Temple. No one knows the real reason for this action. It may have been to win his people's loyalty, to give men work, or perhaps to satisfy a secret ambition to be as great as the ruler of bygone days who built the First Temple. Doubtless the Temple, which had been built by the exiles who returned from Babylonia and was now five hundred years old, did not suit his ideas of grandeur.

The Temple of Herod was truly magnificent. It was begun in the year 20 B.C.E. Only priests worked on building the Temple itself. It took a year and a half to complete the inside of the Temple. Then, thousands of artisans and laborers continued to work on the outer walls and the large outside courts.

It was actually finished many years after, in 64 C.E., only six years before it was destroyed, long after Herod's death.

The Temple could be seen from far and wide, a beautiful edifice of marble and gold. Its great courts admitted thousands of worshippers. The gates to the courts were of fine architecture and fashioned of rich bronze or with gold ornamentation. One spectacular gate was the gift of a wealthy Jew from Alexandria. In spite of its splendor, it was like the earlier, more humble building which it replaced, in one way. Its inmost shrine was the small, unadorned Holy of Holies. The Temple was surrounded by a strong wall. The wall made it a fortress as well as a place of worship.

When the main Temple gates were in place, Herod insulted his people and their religion by placing a golden Roman eagle above the gates for all to see. Years later, when Herod lay dying, a band of Pharisees tried to tear down the eagle. Even then, almost with his dying breath, Herod ordered them to be killed.

Thus, Herod, cruel and ruthless, ruled in Jerusalem. Visitors from other countries, especially non-Jews who did not know or understand the just complaints of the people against Herod, were impressed by the imposing buildings, new palaces, and even whole cities which Herod erected. Because of his building activities, and because his reign was a period of prosperity, he is often called "Herod the Great."

However, the good years began long before his reign, during the days when Simon's sons and grandsons added to the size and wealth of the country. Great cities, flourishing farms, and busy seaports were found in the land when Herod came to the throne, and continued to develop during his rule.

Above all, Herod could take no credit for the intense religious life which flourished during these years.

A FIVE-MINUTE PLAY

Act out the last few minutes of the scene in the Great Sanhedrin. You will need:

Members of the Sanhedrin
King Hyrcanus
Shemayah
One rabbi to state the charge against Herod
Herod and his bodyguard

Select these actors and give them five minutes to talk over their action before they present their play.

TALK OVER IN CLASS

Should a ruler who makes an outward display of large buildings, fine parks, and good roads be considered great?

What other tests should be used before he is called "the great"?

Examine the picture of Herod's Temple in *The Jewish Festivals* by Schauss, p. 131, or in *The Story of the Jewish People* by Jack M. Myers, p. 54.

READ

Hillel by Pilchik, "The More Torah the More Life," p. 1.

Israel Tales and Legends by Arnold Posy, "The Faithful Wife," p. 167.

Great Jewish Women by Elma Ehrlich Levinger, "Mariamne," p. 81.

5. STRONGER THAN THE KING

JERUSALEM was the heart of Jewish religious life in the world. During Queen Salome's reign, the Pharisees were established as the religious leaders. From that time on, though there were Sadducees in the Sanhedrin, Pharisaic interpretations of the Torah were followed.

One of the important duties of the Great Sanhedrin was to decide on the dates of the new moon and the festivals, as well as the dates of the important holidays of the New Year and Yom Kippur. This was called "fixing the calendar."

The Hebrew calendar is based on both the moon and the sun. The number of days in each month depends on the time from one new moon to another, about twenty-nine and one-half days. Because we cannot have half-days on a calendar, some months have thirty days and some have twenty-nine. This makes a year of three hundred and fifty-four days. The sun year has three hundred and sixty-five days. To keep the calendar correct, every second or third year has to be a leap year. In a leap year, an extra month is added. The Sanhedrin had a special method of calculating the leap years. At first it was based on the time when crops ripened. Later it became more accurate, when astronomy, which explains the orderly movement of the stars, the sun, and the moon, was also used.

The dates of the holidays depended on the appearance of the new moon. Two reliable witnesses watched for the new moon, and when they saw it they reported it immediately to the president of the Sanhedrin. Then fires were lit on the highest hills in Jerusalem to signal neighboring cities. When the signal was seen, a fire was lit on the next high hill, and thus in turn every city learned that a new month had begun. For distant communities the news came by messengers who rode by donkey or mule. Outside of Palestine, there was always a little uncertainty about the date of the new moon, and so the custom grew, in those countries, of celebrating two days for holidays and for the beginning of some new months. The responsibility for deciding dates was given to the Great Sanhedrin.

The rulings of the Sanhedrin on Jewish law and on the calendar were followed wherever Jews lived in countries outside of Palestine—in Egypt, in Syria, in Babylonia, and in Rome. Jews in these lands paid the Temple tax regularly. It was collected by a representative in their community and sent to Jerusalem. When Jews in Babylonia or in Egypt had a difficult question on Jewish law, they might write for help to the Sanhedrin. In turn, the Sanhedrin would let the heads of Jewish communities know if they came to an important decision or made a change in the interpretation of a Biblical law.

Many visitors came to Jerusalem to celebrate the festivals, especially the holidays of Sukos, Passover, and Shovuos. These were called Sholosh R'golim, the three Pilgrim Festivals. Jews from other lands longed to see Jerusalem, the city of Zion. Caravans of visitors came year after year. The news of the magnificent Temple of Herod must have spurred on

many more pilgrims. They came from the villages and towns of Palestine, and from countries beyond sea and desert. There were well-kept roads between Babylonia and Jerusalem for pilgrims to travel. They rode on camels and on donkeys, in ox carts or chariots. Many of them came on foot, wearing stout sandals and sturdy robes to last the journey. They traveled in bands to protect themselves against robbers who might waylay them on the road. This was necessary, for they brought with them the Temple tax which often amounted to very large sums. They came to see the Temple, to watch the sacrifices, and to follow the processions of priests and Levites on their way to their appointed Temple tasks. The crowds were so large that the ceremonies often had to be repeated three times in order for all to see them.

The spirit of the country during the festivals was joyful. Those who lived in the land eagerly took the trip to Jerusalem every year or, if possible, for each festival.

Each holiday had its own customs. Shovuos is a good example of a joyful festival. Palestinians who were about to visit Jerusalem would gather at certain central points. They would march together with music to the Holy City. They carried baskets decorated with wreaths and garlands. These baskets contained the offerings of the first fruits, of the seven kinds mentioned in the Bible—wheat, barley, grapes, figs, pomegranates, olives, and honey. The pilgrims were met by priests as they approached the city. When they reached the outer court of the Temple, Levites welcomed the procession by singing the thirtieth psalm, which ends with the words, "O Lord my God, I will give thanks unto Thee forever."

For the pilgrims from far away, the festivals were great occasions. Some of them had waited many years for their visit to Jerusalem.

Visitors who came for the holy day of Yom Kippur would see the High Priest, dressed in his ceremonial robes of white, wan and pale after a wakeful night spent in lonely prayer, go into the Holy of Holies. He was the only man who was permitted to enter that sacred place, and he made his solemn entrance only once a year, on Yom Kippur.

On this important day, the people rejoiced when the High Priest was a man of honor and wisdom whom they respected, and were sad when he was one who had been appointed by the king or the Roman governor in exchange for costly gifts.

A visitor would remain a while in the country. In Jerusalem he would visit the Court of Justice and see the rabbis of the Sanhedrin. He would go to the market-places and buy some of the products of the country—dates and figs, wine, fine oil, wool, and spices. He would purchase some of the articles made by the craftsmen—a bracelet, a woven scarf, or perhaps a decorated plate of metal. A learned man would visit one of the scribes and discuss with him the interpretation of a law, or attend a school where young men were taught the meaning of the Torah. If he could, he would crowd into the room where Hillel or Shammai was speaking to his disciples.

Families would be united for a few days and old friends would plan for future meetings. Merchants would meet other traders and business ventures were begun. In towns and villages outside of Jerusalem, the newcomers would attend synagogue services, and no doubt compare them with their own. By this time, the synagogue was an important institution. It was the center of the religious life of the people. It did not have the same function as the Temple. That was the national shrine of the country. When men went to the synagogue, they heard readings from the Five Books of Moses and from the Prophets. Prayers, the Psalms, and other Bible readings became familiar to all the people through the synagogue and through the Pharisee teachers. The synagogue was the place where any important activity of a town or village was conducted. It had a threefold purpose: to be a Beis ha-T'filo, a house of prayer; a Beis ha-K'nesses, a house of meeting; and a Beis ha-Midrash, a house of study. On market days in Jerusalem, which were Monday and Thursday, the Torah was taken out during the synagogue service and read to the crowds which gathered to listen. From this comes the custom, which is still observed in Orthodox synagogues, of taking the Torah from the Ark on Mondays and Thursdays, as well as on the Sabbath, and reading a portion of the Law.

The leading part which Palestine Jewry played in the religious life of Jews in other countries is emphasized by the full and busy schools which attracted young students from countries outside of Palestine. One of the greatest teachers of the period, whose words are quoted even in our own day, was Hillel. Hillel was a Babylonian Jew who came to Jerusalem as a youthful student to learn the interpretation of the Torah from the rabbis. So wise and learned did he become that he was later appointed president of the Sanhedrin.

Hillel is known as the gentle sage who said, "What is hateful to thee, do not do unto thy neighbor." He believed that Torah—all Jewish learning—was summed up in that one sentence. All the laws and regulations of the Torah were interpretations and explanations of that idea.

Other sayings of Hillel have come down to us. One of them is, "Do not separate thyself from the community." From this we can see how Hillel was eager to have a united people, all working together for their religion and their country.

At another time he declared, "Love peace, seek peace, love mankind; in this way lead them to the Law." He also said, "Do not say, I shall study when I have leisure; perhaps you may never have the leisure."

Under Hillel's great scholarship and wise guidance certain principles regarding the Oral Law were developed. Hillel agreed with the Sadducees that the basis of Jewish law was the regulations as they were found in the Five Books of Moses. As a Pharisee, he went further. He felt that a written law was only a dry and lifeless statement. To make it live and work in the life of the people something more was necessary. The idea behind the law had to be discovered. The laws of the Bible had to be understood so that they would help the people.

He laid down seven principles to guide the rabbis in their decisions. For example, one of the principles was, "If the law applies in an easy case, then it can be used to lead up to a more difficult case." The rabbis could check their decisions against Hillel's principles to see if they were following along the lines laid down by their great teacher.

Another famous rabbi of this period was Shammai. Each of these rabbis had many pupils who followed their interpretations of the laws of the Bible. Hillel and Shammai are usually paired together. In explaining a law, Hillel would be gentle, but Shammai was stern. Hillel tried to make it possible for poor folk to observe the laws. He kept their needs in mind. Shammai's followers came mostly from the wealthier families. In later years the phrase, "according to Hillel," was used most frequently when an explanation was given by a rabbi. Hillel's love of his fellow men was carried forward in Jewish life in the generations that followed.

These were the days when Judea lost its importance as a political power, although it kept its place as the center of religious life. Herod died. His three sons took over the country under Roman supervision. His oldest son was named Ethnarch of Judea, while the other two became governors of Galilee and of the northeastern portion of the land.

Once again a delegation of Jews vainly begged the emperor to permit a High Priest to rule the country. They promised to be loyal to Rome. But the emperor would not listen to them. There were too many centers of rebellion for him to feel safe without his own emissary at the head of the country.

At this very time, spiritual ties with other lands grew stronger. Schools and academies of higher learning became more numerous. Scribes, teachers, and rabbis were respected. The laws and traditions of the Jews were strengthened by the Oral Law which helped the common man to follow ancient law and traditions. Visitors from foreign lands went home impressed by the active Jewish religious life which they saw in Palestine.

SOME QUESTIONS TO ANSWER

Which are the pilgrim festivals?
Do we celebrate any of them today?
Whose way of explaining the Law was generally followed?
What was the idea behind his rulings?
What connections did Jews of other lands have with Judea?
Bring to class an English calendar and a Hebrew calendar.
Which calendar is regulated by the sun?
Which by the sun and the moon?
How many months does each have?
Look up your birthday in the Hebrew calendar.
Look up the date of next Rosh Ha-shono.

READ

The Unconquered by Gaer, "Losers, Winners," p. 300.

Days and Ways by Mamie G. Gamoran, "The Sun—or the Moon," p. 20; "A Whole Day of Prayer," p. 44; "The Festival of First Fruits," p. 149.

The Great March, Book I, by Rose G. Lurie, "School on the Roof," p. 35.

Great Men in Israel by Weis, "The Lost Jewel," p. 7.

Hillel by Pilchik, "The More Righteousness the More Peace," p. 107.

Great Jewish Women by Levinger, "Helena," p. 85.

Unit 2

The Great War

Who could have guessed that in only a few years the whole picture of life in Palestine would change?

No one cause for the change can be given. Many small events led to a crisis. We have to follow these happenings as they occurred, one after another, carrying the nation forward to a tragic decision.

Was war the only way out? Other solutions were offered by different groups in the country. The reasons they had for their own way of thinking explain what happened during the next period.

At the Walls of Jerusalem

6. INTRODUCTION TO WAR

UP TO this time, the letters B.C.E. (Before the Common Era) have been part of our dates. This means, as you remember, that all the events we talked about happened before the Common Era, which began with the year 1. We are living now 1955 or more years after the year 1 C.E. The year 1 is supposed to be the date of the birth of Jesus, of whom you will hear later in this chapter.

The events in our history which follow took place in the Common Era. We have passed over that imaginary line which divides B.C.E. from C.E.

The first date in the Common Era of interest to us is the year 6, when Herod's son was removed from his office of ethnarch. From the year 6 C.E. * until the year 66, with one short exception, the country of Palestine was ruled by Roman officials, called Procurators.

The people as a whole did not mind being a province of Rome's vast empire. Rome played a great role in the history of the world. She brought law and order to many lands. Together, Roman law and Jewish religious ideas might have brought great benefits to the world. But the main idea behind

* From now on, the letters C.E. will be omitted.

Roman conquest was not the spread of civilization; it was power and wealth. Lands were conquered to bring gold and valuable merchandise to Rome and its cities.

Nearly every Roman procurator who came to Jerusalem had but one thought in mind—to get from the land under his rule the most in taxes and fees and gifts that he possibly could, so that after sending a share to Rome, a goodly sum would remain with him. He did not have in mind the welfare of the people; they were only a source of gain to his treasury. He usually tried to have friendly relations with the wealthy men, for they could help him. He did not mind offending the large masses of people. One of the procurators kept the robes of the High Priest under lock and key. When the High Priest wanted to officiate in the Temple, he had to come and ask for his robes. The office of High Priest was completely under the control of the procurator.

During these years many changes took place. Heavy taxes for the support of Roman officials and the Roman soldiers were levied. Customs duties took large sums of money. These became a great burden on the people. The wealth of the country began to pass into fewer and fewer hands. Instead of many small farm holdings, a good part of the land was the property of large landowners. They rented out their acreage to tenants who paid for the land in produce and labor. In some ways, conditions were similar to those in the Kingdom of Israel when the prophet, Amos, preached. Some farmers who lost their land because of taxes or poor years came to the cities and looked for work. Many men could not earn enough to take care of their families.

Once during a year of famine the poor of Jerusalem were helped in an unexpected way. They received large quantities of food from a visiting queen. This is what happened.

In the plains of Mesopotamia was the small kingdom of Adiabene. The king of Adiabene was named Izates. Izates had been sent away from home during his boyhood to another kingdom. Like the prince in a fairy tale, he married the king's daughter. A Jewish merchant came to the court. While he sold his wares, he told of his religion. He must have been an excellent speaker, for he converted many of the members of the court to Judaism, including Izates, the prince, and his wife, Samach, the princess.

When Izates was called back to Adiabene to assume the throne, he continued his interest in Judaism. He studied the Bible with the help of a Jew from Galilee who came to Adiabene. Izates learned on his return home that his mother, the Queen Helena, had also been converted to Judaism. Thus the two most important people in the kingdom, the king and the Queen Mother, became Jews. Others in the royal family followed their example.

Queen Helena, just like other faithful Jews, longed to see the Temple. At last, she and Izates set out on a journey to Jerusalem. She presented a fine gold ornament to the Temple.

It was placed on one of the Temple doors in such a way as to reflect the very first rays of the morning sun. When the priests saw the reflection, they knew that the dawn had arrived, and the morning service should begin.

Helena came to Jerusalem at the time of a severe famine. People were starving and ill from lack of food. She was a woman of action as well as of spiritual devotion. She sent for great cargoes of wheat and figs from Egypt and Cyprus. As soon as they arrived, she gave food to all in need.

Later on, Izates sent five of his sons to Jerusalem to receive a Jewish education. He wanted them to be Jews in deed as well as in name. When Queen Helena and King Izates died, their bodies were brought in state to Jerusalem and they were buried on the outskirts of the Holy City.

But Queen Helena's help against the famine could not change the tide of events. Bitter feeling arose against the Roman overlords and also against the wealthy Jews who seemed to be satisfied with Roman rule.

Some men were determined to rebel against Rome. They wanted independence again. They realized how dearly it had been bought by the Maccabees and how easily it had slipped through the hands of their descendants. These people were called Zealots. They bided their time but were always in the center of small uprisings which took place, especially in Galilee, at this time. Hezekiah and his followers, for whose murder Herod was brought to trial, were early Zealots. Many years later Hezekiah's son, Judah, fought bravely against Roman legions, and kept a large part of Galilee under his control.

On the other hand, many of the leaders among the Pharisees felt that the Jews must come to terms with the Romans. They wanted peace. They had given up hopes of political independence. Their ideals were study, love of God, and the opportunity to live the kind of life commanded by the Torah. This was the group which had sent the embassy to Rome to ask to be ruled by a High Priest under Roman supervision.

What was the best course to take? Should the Jews continue under procurators, because this served the purposes of the wealthy group? Should they compromise, so that schools might continue and Jewish tradition flourish? Was it to be rebellion and war—a fight for Jewish political and spiritual independence?

These were some of the different ways in which the difficult problems which faced the Jews might have been solved. But a new element came into the picture. Many people, especially those who were very poor, dreamed of a great leader who would come to help them. They were ready to listen to anyone who came with a promise to make life better and easier.

From this turmoil, from these desperate needs, came strange events. They were destined to turn the religion of a great part of the world into new channels, and to leave their mark forever on Jewish history.

In Galilee, a wandering preacher named Jochanan, or John, appeared. He declared that the time was near for a Messiah to come. The idea of the Messiah was not new in Jewish tra-

dition. One of Isaiah's greatest prophecies was taken to be a proclamation that some day a Messiah would appear. Isaiah said:

> And there shall come forth a shoot out of the stock of
> Jesse, . . .
> And the spirit of the Lord shall rest upon him,
> The spirit of wisdom and understanding, . . .
> The spirit of knowledge and of the fear of the
> Lord. . . .
> With righteousness shall he judge the poor,
> And decide with equity for the meek of the land; . . .
> And the wolf shall dwell with the lamb,
> And the leopard shall lie down with the kid;
> And the calf and the young lion and the fatling together;
> And a little child shall lead them. . . .
> They shall not hurt nor destroy
> In all My holy mountain;
> For the earth shall be full of the knowledge of the
> Lord,
> As the waters cover the sea.

The Messiah was to be a man, a descendant of David, who was to bring to the world an era of peace, of plenty, and of love for God and man.

Jochanan was a figure something like Elijah, coming out of the desert, wearing a single robe caught with a belt. He was probably one of the Essenes and he attracted many followers. At his bidding they plunged into the waters of the Jordan. This ceremony was called baptism. John declared that baptism cleansed his followers of their sins and made them ready for the Kingdom of God.

Among the followers of John the Baptist was a young man

of Nazareth named Joshua. His Greek name was Jesus, and that is how he is known to the world today.

Jochanan displeased Herod's son, Antipas, ruler of Galilee. To the rulers of the land, anyone who was the leader of a group was dangerous. It was always possible that he was gathering forces for a rebellion. For this and other reasons, Jochanan was executed.

Before long, Jesus had taken the place of Jochanan and was well known among the poorer families near and around Nazareth. Jesus was a Jew, and he spoke to his listeners as one Jew to another. He used quotations from the Torah and the Prophets, and the words of the great teachers like Hillel. However, he sometimes changed them in a way which did not please the Pharisees and the scribes when they heard about it.

Jesus spoke differently from any other teacher and from the prophets whose words he used. The prophets, for example, always said, "Thus saith the Lord," or "The Lord spoke unto me, saying." The prophet was always the spokesman of God.

Jesus often began his preaching by saying, "I say unto you." He spoke in his own name, but he expected his words to carry the same weight as the words of the prophets and teachers.

Jesus became known as a healer, and his help was sought for many sick people. Gradually he gathered around him a group of followers. Some called him the "Messiah." Others even whispered he was a "son of God."

Just before Passover, Jesus and his followers, like so many other Jews, decided to visit the Temple in Jerusalem for the holiday. The story of Jesus' visit to Jerusalem, as it has come down to us, is a blend of some facts and many legends.

After his arrival in Jerusalem, Jesus visited the Temple. He became angry to see money changers in one of the Temple courts. He did not realize they were there to change money for foreign pilgrims. Jesus drove out the money changers and upset their tables and chairs. There was a small riot in the Temple court that day.

Jesus was arrested. When he was questioned, he declared he was the Messiah. Some believed he was king of the Jews. In the eyes of the Romans, declarations like these were crimes against the State. Jesus' actions threatened to bring trouble to Jerusalem. He was brought before Pontius Pilate, the procurator, for judgment.

Pontius Pilate was one of the cruelest procurators who ever ruled in Judea. He was known for his violence and ill treatment of the people. More than once he executed without trial men whom he suspected of rebelling against Rome. The disturbance caused by Jesus and his followers in the city was hateful to the procurator. To him, Jesus was another rebel against Rome. He condemned Jesus to death by the cruel Roman method of crucifixion.

So Jesus of Nazareth died. He was a victim of the unrest of his times—an unhappy period in Jewish history.

Jesus' followers did not forget him. Many stories and legends grew up about him and his teachings. More people joined the small band of faithful believers. Years later Saul, a Jew of Tarsus, made Jesus the central figure of a new religion. This religion, Christianity, was like a branch grafted on to a living tree. It grew, drawing its sap from the original tree.

At this time, however, the story of Jesus seemed only an incident on the troubled surface.

A few years of quiet brought new hope for peaceful days. A Jew name Agrippa, who was the grandson of Herod, was appointed king of Judea. Later the Roman emperor gave him the provinces of Galilee, Samaria, and Idumea, so that for a few years he ruled over a large and united Palestine.

King Agrippa took his task seriously. He remembered that he was a grandson of Mariamne, a Maccabean. As soon as he came to Jerusalem, he presented to the Temple a golden chain which he had received as a gift from the Roman emperor. He observed Jewish religious life and traditions and

took part in the ceremonies of worship and sacrifice. He prevented the emperor from carrying out a threat to place his statue in the Temple.

Agrippa had his enemies who watched his every move. When he began to build a wall around Jerusalem to make the city stronger, he had to stop suddenly on orders from

Rome. The governor of Syria had sent word that aroused the suspicions of the emperor.

Agrippa died suddenly, as was often the case in those days when a ruler was too capable and too humane. From then on, after the year 44, the story of cruel and greedy procurators was repeated again and again.

The proud, freedom-loving Jews would not forever remain crushed by oppression. They were slowly coming to the breaking point. The Romans found new ways to hurt them. Not only was their political freedom taken away; the rulers began to interfere with their religious life. The heavy taxes continued year after year. All over the country there were muttering, uprisings, outbreaks. The spark of liberty was soon to burst forth into a great flame.

SOMETHING TO THINK ABOUT

Read over the quotation from Isaiah on page 48.

Write down what the prophet thought would happen after the Messiah appeared.

Who was Jesse? Who was his most famous "shoot"?

Why did some Pharisees believe with many Sadducees that it would be best not to start a war with Rome?

READINGS FOR TEACHERS

Unit 2 (*CHAPTERS 6–8*)

A History of the Jews by Grayzel, Chap. IX.

A History of the Jewish People by Margolis and Marx, Chaps. XXX, XXXI, and XXXII.

Jewish Literature Since the Bible, Book I, by Leon I. Feuer, "The Fall of Jerusalem" by Flavius Josephus, p. 7.

7. FIGHTING IN GALILEE

IN THE year 66, Florus governed Judea. He was the last procurator. His actions brought about the change from dissatisfaction to active rebellion.

Florus took his share of the regular taxes. This was not enough for him. He greedily extended his hand to rob Temple funds, which were sent in with love and loyalty by all Jews. These were used to keep the Temple in good order, to purchase sacrifices, and to supply the needs of the priests and Levites. The people were outraged. They showed their anger by making fun of Florus. As though he were a beggar, they passed baskets in the streets, "For Florus, the poor Procurator."

The Roman governor was furious. He set his soldiers on the crowds which had assembled, and almost a thousand people were slain. A short time later two Roman regiments entered Jerusalem. Florus declared he would accept only one peace offering—the people must extend the hand of friendship to the soldiers. With bitter hearts the people accepted the decree. But the Roman soldiers did not reply to the greeting as they entered the city. No doubt there were insults, shouts, and quarrels. Soon there was a real battle in the streets.

Some Jews still hoped to find a way to live with Rome. For a few days, two parties fought in Jerusalem. Was it to be peace or war? The Zealots who wanted war gathered their

forces and barricaded themselves in the Temple fortress. They won out. The peace party, led by the son of King Agrippa, wealthy nobles, priests, and some leading Pharisees, left the city in the hands of the Zealots and their followers. The Roman soldiers were completely wiped out.

This did not go unnoticed in Rome, or even nearer, in Syria, where the governor of the entire area lived. The governor came southward with many troops to crush the revolution, as he thought, in a few days. On his way down through the country, he fell on villages and towns. Many he destroyed; others he looted. At last, just a few days after Sukos, he reached Jerusalem.

The city was full. The people gathered for a battle. Pilgrims from other lands who still remained in Jerusalem stood by their brethren. They put up a good fight. For five days the Romans stormed the walls. At last they made a small break, but their commander realized he could not follow up this advantage. Autumn was coming with the rainy season. He had lost many men. He could be trapped in the hands of the Jews. He fell back. As he retreated he was followed and attacked by Jewish forces. The Romans fled in the night, leaving behind valuable stores of food, ammunition, and even money. They lost almost six thousand men. To add to their crushing defeat, they also lost their standards, the Roman eagles, sign of imperial Rome. The first battle was a complete victory for the Zealots.

A real war strategy had to be planned. Even now there was no complete unity. Almost a hundred years had passed since the Jews had had political leadership in their own hands. From the time of Herod they had had foreign masters. No wonder that now, plunged into war, they were disorganized and unready. But they knew what they wanted. As one mark of rebellion, they stopped the daily sacrifice which had been made in the name of the emperor. No longer would a Temple flame burn to honor a Roman ruler.

The question of the day was, who could lead the Jewish forces? The Jews pinned their hopes on a young man who gave every promise of being a fine leader. He proved to be a tragic disappointment. His name was Josephus. Josephus was appointed military governor of Galilee, the northern section of Palestine. The leaders believed, and they were right, that the first attack would come on Galilee. Galilee was a rich, fertile area. If Galilee held out it could supply food for man and beast. The longer Galilee remained strong, the longer Roman forces would be prevented from marching on to Jerusalem.

In our day we would say, "Josephus played it safe." He did as little as possible to prepare Galilee for the Roman invasion. He did not unite his men into one strong fighting force. He wanted to be able to prove to Rome that he had really been on their side. For Josephus had been to Rome, and he envied its power and its might. In his heart of hearts he did not expect the Jews to be victorious. This half-hearted leader was the military governor of the province which was to hold back invincible Rome!

Some leaders suspected Josephus. They sent some men to see what he was doing, and tried to remove him from his office. Josephus managed to hold on to his position even though he was unworthy of it. Those who opposed him in Galilee were led by John of Gischala, a fighting patriot.

In Rome, the emperor realized that the Jews were in earnest. He selected his best general, named Vespasian, to put down the rebellion. Vespasian had conquered the sturdy Britons and the war-like Germans. He was experienced and able.

With sixty thousand trained soldiers and a goodly store of fresh supplies, Vespasian came down from Syria, through Galilee. The Jews fought bravely in small groups under patri-

otic leaders. In spite of the poor preparations which Josephus had made, his men withstood Vespasian. It took him a whole year to break through their lines and move on southward. But stout hearts alone could not overcome greater numbers and better arms.

The last battle was fought in the fortress of Jotapata. The Jews held out against the superior forces and the better weapons of the Romans for forty-seven days. At last, only forty men were left, hidden in a cistern. Willingly or unwillingly, Josephus was among them. The soldiers made a pact, never to surrender. When they saw they had to give up or die, they decided to die. They drew lots to determine the order in which they would die, one by one, at the hands of their comrades. All but Josephus. Clever to the end, he managed to remain alive until only he and one last soldier were left. He overpowered this man and surrendered to the Romans. Though he was a prisoner, he was treated well. From that time on, he assisted the Romans.

Josephus closed his eyes to the fact that he had paved the way for the fall of his country. Years later, safe in Rome under the protection of the emperor, he calmly told of his deeds when he wrote two large histories of the Jewish people. One is called the *Antiquities of the Jews*. The other is named *The Wars of the Jews*. From these volumes we have first-hand and in some cases eye-witness stories of the war with Rome. Much as he is to be despised for his treachery and cowardice, Josephus' work as historian has been invaluable to all students of Jewish history.

Down to Jerusalem came the Roman forces. Refugees from villages and towns came flocking to the sacred city. They believed with all their hearts that Zion, the city of David, could never be taken. It was indeed a stronghold. Three great walls surrounded the city, which the Romans would have to break down before they could enter.

Inside the city there was confusion. No single leader had come forth to unite all the people. John of Gischala had a large following. Other leaders had groups which listened to them. There were quarrels among the different parties. A great store of grain, saved for the very purpose of withstanding a siege, was burned through such a quarrel. This foreshadowed what was to become a serious problem. The defenders of the city might have withstood the attacks of the Romans, but they had no weapons against hunger and starvation.

However, there came a lull in the fighting which lasted two years. Vespasian withdrew his troops to Caesarea and left for Rome. He hoped to become emperor, and before long his hopes were realized. He was crowned king. These years might have been spent in strengthening the city and disciplining the soldiers, but no one leader was able to rally a united force. The opportunity was lost.

Then once again the Romans were outside Jerusalem.

SOME TOPICS TO WRITE ABOUT

You suspect Josephus is not preparing well for the Roman invasion. You write to an important official in Jerusalem and ask him to investigate.

You are the leader of one of the groups in Jerusalem. Write to one of the other leaders and ask him to unite with you. Give him the advantages of working together.

You are the governor of Syria who came down to fight in Jerusalem. Write a letter to Rome telling why you fled from Jerusalem, even though your men had begun to make a break in the wall.

8. THE FALL OF THE TEMPLE

VESPASIAN, the new Roman emperor, placed his son Titus in command of the siege of Jerusalem. Both Vespasian and Titus were determined to use every means at their command to crush the Judeans. Titus arrived with his forces just before Passover, in the year 70.

Titus had no guns or cannon, but he had other mighty weapons to break down the walls of Jerusalem. His chief weapon was the ballista. This was like the sling-shot of David, enlarged to gigantic size. It could throw a rock weighing over a hundred pounds as far as a quarter of a mile. Titus' men gathered these enormous stones and painted them white. As the rocks sped through the air, they could easily be watched to see if each found its mark. In addition to the ballista, Titus used great battering-rams. Josephus describes the battering-rams in the following words—the words of one who saw and was awed by these mighty weapons:

> "This battering-ram is a vast beam of wood like the mast of a ship; its forepart is armed with a thick piece of iron at the head of it, which is carved like the head of a ram, from which its name is taken. This ram is

slung in the air by ropes passing over its middle, and is hung like the balance in a pair of scales from another beam, and braced by strong beams that pass on both sides of it, something like a cross. When this ram is pulled backward by a great number of men with united force, and then thrust forward by the same men, with a mighty noise, it batters the walls with that iron part which is in front, and there is no tower so strong, or walls so broad, that can resist any more than its first batteries. All are forced to yield to it at last."

For these machines, the Romans cut down the largest trees which grew around Jerusalem. Other trees they cut down for their towers. Not a tree was left standing for ten miles around Jerusalem. Day after day, the battering-rams and the ballista did their deadly damage. And every day, the unseen ally, starvation, grew stronger and stronger.

During the months of siege, Titus called on the Jews to surrender. At his side, as he made his plea, was Josephus, now one of the Roman general's advisers.

At last, but too late, the Jews were united. They would never give up Jerusalem. They fought courageously. Women joined their husbands and brothers to fight. The huge stones sent over by the ballista were thrown back upon the enemy. But time and numbers were on the side of the Romans.

The first and then the second wall were broken through. Still the Jews held their ground in their last stronghold, the Temple fortress. They were united behind two great fighters, John of Gischala and Simon bar Giora.

On the 17th of Tamuz, that is in our month of July, defeat was near. On that day, for the first time, the priests had to give up the daily sacrifice in the Temple. Nevertheless, the Jews fought grimly on. The great battering-rams hit the walls of the Temple without ceasing. Three more weeks passed. The people were starved and exhausted. Thousands had perished. But the spirit of the survivors was strong.

The Romans closed in. They scaled the crumbling walls, to be beaten back, to try again, and to fall back once more. At last one of their number threw a flaming torch into the Temple.

The 9th of Ov, the date which marked the destruction of the First Temple by Nebuchadnezzar, was the day when the Second Temple went up in flames. As the Temple vanished in fire and smoke, the brave, almost superhuman resistance of the Jews came to an end. Jerusalem fell to Rome.

How many died that day, both Roman and Jew, no one will know. The savage Roman troops spared no one. In the mad fighting that followed, the Romans seized many of the sacred vessels and ornaments of the Temple. These vessels were the outward symbols of their hard-won conquest of Jerusalem, and they were valuable spoils of a war which had been very costly in money, goods, and men. The Temple treasury yielded many gold and silver objects used in the Temple service. Gifts presented by pious pilgrims over the course of years, as well as vast stores of gold and money, were kept in the treasury. All went to Rome.

The life and death struggle of Rome and Jerusalem had been watched by Rome and its far-flung provinces. How had the tiny forces of the Jews withstood Titus' mighty army for so long? When Titus returned to Rome, it was important to him to flaunt his victory before the Roman people. Hundreds of Jewish captives marched in his triumphal procession through the streets of the capital. At their head, in chains, marched John of Gischala and Simon bar Giora, who had continued fighting even after the Temple was destroyed.

Titus gloried in his conquest of Judea. The Romans built a great marble arch in Rome to mark his victory. On the inner wall of the arch the workmen carved pictures of the Jewish

captives and the vessels taken from the Temple. The Romans must have thought that this arch would be a final memorial to a people lost forever to the conqueror's might.

How mistaken they were! The Arch of Titus still stands near the Roman Forum, and curious tourists visit it every day. It is a lasting memorial not to a dead and forgotten nation, but to a living people whose teachers and prophets are part of the civilization of the world.

Titus could not guess that during the very days when Roman soldiers were preparing to overcome Jerusalem, Jewish teachers were taking steps to keep alive Jewish teachings and traditions, and through them, the Jewish people.

SOMETHING TO DO

Make a list of all the ancient nations you can think of. Which are still living today? Which have passed away?

SOMETHING TO TALK OVER IN CLASS

The prophet, Zechariah, said, "Not by might, nor by power, but by My spirit, saith the Lord of hosts."

Use this sentence as a starting point to explain why some very strong nations of long ago have passed away.

Examine the picture of the Arch of Titus on p. 63.

Which is stronger, the Temple which went up in flames, or the Arch of Titus which still stands? Why?

READ

The Great March, Book I, by Lurie, "Enough for Wash Day," p. 62.

Unit 3

The Last Stand

Wars may kill men, but the ideals they fought for live on. Thousands of Jews—men, women, and children—had been killed, deported, and enslaved.

Encouragement, help, and guidance were needed if Jewish life was to be set on a firm foundation once more.

Warriors had failed. Again the Jews turned to those who had led them since the days of Ezra—the teachers and rabbis.

Could they prove equal to the task which faced them? What did they achieve?

Rabbi and General

9. THE SCHOOL AT JABNEH

THE ASSYRIANS exiled the Israelites and sent men and women of other conquered nations to take over the land of Israel. The Babylonians exiled the Judeans but permitted them to live as a group in Babylonia. The Romans did something else.

They took with them to Rome a few hundred of the most handsome Jewish youths to march in Titus' triumphal procession. These captives were only a symbol of Rome's victory. Eventually most of them were probably ransomed by Jews who lived in Rome. Other thousands of Jews were sent as slaves to the copper mines of the Sinai desert, to live out a wretched life in that cheerless area. Many men were pitted against gladiators and wild beasts in savage contests in the arenas of Caesarea for the entertainment of Titus and his guests. But the majority of Jews were neither exiled from Judea nor enslaved. They remained in their land amid the ruins left by war.

Jerusalem was in ruins but in the rest of the country hundreds of villages, towns, and cities stood as before. True, many young men were gone forever, lost in the great war. Fields had been spoiled and flocks stolen by marching soldiers. The country was no longer a semi-independent province of Rome. A Roman governor ruled directly from Caesarea, without Jewish officials or advisers.

In other ways the inhabitants of the land found their lives had changed. No longer could the white and golden towers of the Temple beckon to them from afar. No longer could they think of the daily sacrifice which for so many years they had shared, by sending gifts and visiting the Temple. They learned, perhaps to their surprise, that Jewish life would continue without the Temple, without sacrifices, without the High Priest. Though these were lost, the strong foundation of the laws of the Bible, the ideals of the prophets, and the teachings of the rabbis still remained. These meant life, faith, and hope.

During the final period of the siege of Jerusalem, a scholar sat in the shadow of the Temple. To him came students, Pharisaic leaders, and scribes. He taught the students, and with the older men discussed the serious state of affairs. He believed that a way should be found to live as a Jewish community under Roman rule. It must have been hard to keep apart from the clashes of war. The Zealots must have called to the students to leave the house of study and to join the rebellion.

This scholar and teacher, Rabbi Jochanan ben Zakkai, had his own plans for overcoming Rome, and his weapons were neither arrows, nor spears, nor javelins.

One day a group of students appeared at one of the gates of Jerusalem. They carried on their shoulders a coffin which held the body of their respected teacher, Jochanan ben Zakkai. They asked the guards to allow them to leave the city to bury their teacher. The guards permitted them to leave.

Jochanan ben Zakkai was not dead. Only by such a ruse

could he have left Jerusalem. Once beyond the city gates, he was taken from the coffin. Then he went to the tent of the Roman commander. Titus knew through his spies that Jochanan was a member of the peace party. He did not know, however, why the rabbi begged the citizens of Jerusalem to make peace with the Romans. He could not guess that in Jochanan ben Zakkai he had an adversary over whom arms and weapons of war would not prevail.

The Roman general wanted to be kind and generous to the aged rabbi. He was eager to give him some special mark of favor. Jochanan ben Zakkai made only a simple request. He asked permission to go to the seaport town of Jabneh to start a school there. Without question, Titus granted this request. It may have seemed even a little foolish to him.

The school in Jabneh was a reality when the Temple was destroyed. The men who had gathered there were ready to cope with the serious questions which arose at that time. What of the sacrifices—what of the many ceremonies and statutes which depended on the Temple and on Jerusalem—what of the Sanhedrin?

For the first question, Jochanan ben Zakkai had an excellent reply. He said to his students who wept when they heard the awful news that the Temple was burnt, "Do not weep. Charity will take the place of sacrifice!" He quoted the words of the prophet Hosea who said that God declared, "I take pleasure in mercy and not in burnt offerings."

To help answer the other questions, Jochanan organized a court of justice in Jabneh which was called the Sanhedrin. This court became the official body for dealing with all problems except those few which were taken care of by Roman officials. Taxes which had to be paid to Rome and questions regarding ownership of the land were in Roman hands. All other aspects of daily living were under the guidance of the Sanhedrin in Jabneh and were regulated by Jewish law.

The Sanhedrin in Jabneh was composed of Pharisaic teachers and rabbis. After the destruction of the Temple, the Sadducees disappeared from Jewish life. Judaism could continue only if it was ready to change and adjust to the new conditions. The Sadducees with their ideas of unchanging law gave way to the leadership of the Pharisees.

Jabneh was recognized as the center of Jewish religious life in Palestine and in other lands where Jews lived. The dates of the calendar were fixed in Jabneh and accepted in all Jewish communities. The power to fix the calendar carried with it authority on all questions of Jewish law. When the Day of Atonement fell on a Sabbath, the question of blowing the shofor on that day came up. Up to this time, the shofor was never blown on the Sabbath anywhere but in Jerusalem. Would they dare to blow the shofor in Jabneh on the Sabbath? Jochanan ben Zakkai gave the order. The place of Jabneh was settled as a center of law and learning.

Jochanan ben Zakkai was well known as a scholar and a

teacher. Many famous stories of him and his pupils have come down to us. Once he gave them a question to think about. It was, "What should a man try hardest for in his life?"

One pupil answered, "A good eye." One said, "A noble friend." Another replied, "A fine neighbor." The fourth answered, "The power to think through his actions carefully and know what their results will be." The last pupil declared, "A man's best possession is a noble heart." Jochanan praised the last answer, for he felt that with a good heart, a man would be a good friend and a good neighbor. His good heart would bring him other fine qualities.

Jochanan's far-sighted mind looked to the future. First he taught his pupils thoroughly. Then, when they were ready, he ordained them as rabbis; that is, he declared that they were worthy of the title of "Rabbi." Ordination was a solemn ceremony. The rabbi would lay his hands on the head of his young students and bless them. With the title of rabbi it was possible to continue Jochanan's work, and to teach others. Rabbi means "my Master," and is a title of great respect.

From Jabneh, therefore, came an unbroken chain of rabbis and teachers who took the place of leadership which the priests in the Temple and the members of the Sanhedrin had held before in Jerusalem.

Slowly the country struggled to its feet. For a few years after Jerusalem was lost there were some attempts at continued rebellion, but when the last fortress at Masada fell three years later, even the most bitter die-hards realized that further fighting was useless.

Now the work of rebuilding began. In some ways this took greater courage than the fighting. In Galilee the emperor had appointed a Jewish governor. Recovery went on more rapidly there. Galilee had rich land. In addition it had fishing in Lake Chinnereth which brought a livelihood to many families.

Judea was in a bad state. Over a million people had died in the war. Farms could not produce without men to sow the seed and to till the soil. Trade and commerce were at a standstill. Homes and public buildings had to be rebuilt. Even the elements seemed to be against the farmers; for a few years rainfall was scanty and poverty was wide-spread.

The land was now considered to be the property of the Roman Empire. Those who lived on it did not own it. They were merely lessees or renters. Roman soldiers were given parcels of land to settle as a reward for their part in the war. The Temple tax which had gladly been given by every Jewish home in and outside of Palestine was now gathered by Roman tax-collectors. But it went to support the Temple of Jupiter in the city of Rome. This was the bitterest blow of all.

Yet no one despaired. In every tiny hamlet and in each war-torn town the knowledge that in Jabneh the light of the law still burned brightly gave hope to weary men and sad-eyed women.

SOME QUESTIONS TO TALK OVER IN CLASS

What was Rabbi Jochanan's "Secret Weapon"?

What answer would you give to the question, "What should a man try hardest for in his life"?

A FIVE-MINUTE PLAY

Act out a five-minute play about the escape of Rabbi Jochanan ben Zakkai.

You will need:

Roman soldiers
Pupils of the rabbi

(Let Rabbi Jochanan appear from the side after his pupils have passed through Roman lines.)

READ

The Great March, Book I, by Lurie, "The School That Saved a People," p. 52.

Watchmen of the Night by Betty Kalisher, "The Man Who Saved Judaism," p. 1.

READINGS FOR TEACHERS

Unit 3 (*CHAPTERS 9–11*)

A History of the Jews, Book I, by Grayzel, Chap. XII.

Book II, Chap. I.

A History of the Jewish People by Margolis and Marx, Chap. XXXIII.

Jewish Post-Biblical History by Adele Bildersee, "Jochanan ben Zakkai," Chap. I; "Akiba," Chap. II.

The Story of the Jewish People by Myers, Chaps. XXIII-XXIX.

The Patriarchate by Kenneth E. Stein.

10. THE MEN OF THE NEW SANHEDRIN

A MORE interesting group of men than those who were members of the Academy at Jabneh can hardly be imagined. They were a true cross-section of the country. In them the ideal of the Pharisees, that learning should be the possession of every man, seemed to have come true. The scholars at Jabneh were not a priestly class, nor were they men of leisure. Most of them earned their living in trades not associated with their duties at the Sanhedrin. As a matter of fact, teachers and judges were not permitted to receive money for their work. Among the members of the Sanhedrin were some priests, it is true, but others were men of ordinary family and background. Some were craftsmen, tanners, cobblers, or weavers; some were farmers and shepherds; some were wealthy landowners. In the Sanhedrin all were equal. Only scholarship and knowledge of the law could give them prominence.

The president of the Sanhedrin who followed Jochanan ben Zakkai was Gamaliel II, a grandson of Hillel. The first Gamaliel had been the head of the Sanhedrin in Jerusalem. Gamaliel II received the title, "Patriarch," which in time came to be the title of the official head of the entire Jewish community in Palestine. The Roman governor of Syria, of which Palestine was a part, recognized Gamaliel II in his office of patriarch. He held this position between the years of 80 and 110.

Gamaliel II had but one aim. It was the welfare of his people. For this reason he traveled all over the country; to Tiberias in the north, to Samaria, Emmaus, and Lydda in the center, and to Jericho in the south. By personal inspection he noted those places where prosperity was coming again, and those areas in need. He learned where the large funds for charity which had been set up could best be used. In this way, Gamaliel discovered at first hand how his countrymen fared.

But the head of the Sanhedrin could not be satisfied to check only on the physical needs of the people. He examined also schools and synagogues. By this time schools had been opened in other cities besides Jabneh. As far back as the year 64, Joshua ben Gamala, who was the High Priest, ordered schools to be opened in every town and in every province. He also decreed that boys of six and seven should be brought to these schools. Elementary schools for boys and schools

for higher learning were now to be found all over. Some of Jochanan ben Zakkai's pupils were rabbis and teachers in these schools. They taught and explained the law to their pupils. They answered questions which the people brought to them. Often one rabbi might follow the teachings of one teacher, while in a nearby town the Law was interpreted according to the explanation of another rabbi. Usually the explanation followed the rules laid down either by Hillel or by the other great rabbi of his day, Shammai.

Gamaliel saw that unity in Jewish religious life was all-important. He worked through the Sanhedrin. After many discussions, it was finally decided that the Biblical laws were to be interpreted and followed according to the regulations laid down by Hillel. However, a rabbi could add that a different opinion was held by Shammai or by another teacher.

Something like this is the practice in the Supreme Court of the United States. When all nine judges of the Supreme Court do not agree, the minority may issue a statement telling why they disagree with the majority. This is called a "minority report." It is the democratic way of giving every man the right to express his own opinion. This system was followed long ago in the Sanhedrin at Jabneh.

The Sanhedrin under Gamaliel II laid down rules for the synagogue. Its members said that certain prayers, like the Sh'ma, were to be repeated three times a day. They revised a series of prayers, called the "Eighteen Benedictions," which form a part of the traditional daily prayer book to this day. Part of them are included in the Reform prayer book.

We can learn a great deal of history from these prayers. You remember that the Psalms which were written years earlier as beautiful songs described events which had happened. They taught us history. One of the new prayers asked for the restoration of Jerusalem. This prayer had to be written after 70. In Herod's time, for example, no one would have thought of such a prayer. Another section of the Eighteen Benedictions asked God to punish slanderers, but begged Him to be merciful to "righteous converts" to Judaism. From these prayers we understand that enemies were telling evil stories about the Jews. We also learn that numerous non-Jews were accepting Judaism as their religion.

Gamaliel also began the custom of the Seder service, substituting prayer for the Passover sacrifice. This ceremony has come down to our own day.

Gamaliel was so eager for unity that sometimes he went too far. One year, as the month of Tishri approached (that is the month in which Rosh Ha-shono and Yom Kippur occur), the watchers for the new moon reported to him as usual. This time they seem to have made a mistake, and when the patriarch declared that a certain day was the Day of Atonement, one of the rabbis named Joshua ben Chananya disagreed. Gamaliel would permit no one to question his ruling. To prove his point he ordered Joshua to appear before him in working clothes, on the very day which Joshua believed to be Yom Kippur.

At first Joshua would not yield, but his friends urged him to consider that the authority of the patriarch and the Sanhedrin must be kept. Instead of dressing in his white robes on the day which was to him the holiest of the year, Joshua put on his working clothes, and carrying his staff and his money, came before Gamaliel.

Gamaliel realized the great sacrifice Joshua had made. He said, "Welcome, Joshua, my teacher and my pupil. My teacher in wisdom, my pupil in obedience."

At other times, Gamaliel acted without consideration for

the members of the Sanhedrin. At last they met and decided to remove him from his office of president of the Sanhedrin. In his stead, they appointed a young man who was only eighteen years old, but who came from a family of learning, prestige, and wealth.

Gamaliel took his removal from office with good grace. He remained a loyal member of the Sanhedrin and attended meetings regularly. He spoke from his seat among the ordinary members and accepted his new position without rancor.

This display of good character made a great impression on his fellow members. Before long, they once more offered him the position of president. In democratic fashion, a compromise was worked out. Each month, Gamaliel II presided over the Sanhedrin for three weeks, and his successor was president for one week.

During this period the last books of the Bible were accepted into the Canon. They were the Koheleth or Ecclesiastes, the Song of Songs, and the Book of Esther. The first two are called the writings of King Solomon, although Biblical scholars think they were written by later writers. The Book of Esther was placed in the Bible after a great deal of

discussion by the rabbis. The holiday of Purim had been celebrated for many years, going back to the days of the Maccabees. It was a popular festival. At last it was decided that the Book of Esther deserved a place in the Bible.

The selection of scrolls and writings for the Book of Books was begun in the days before Ezra. Over seven hundred years went by before this important task was completed. The Bible was fixed. No more books would be declared holy. No book has been read or studied by more people, and no book has influenced the world more than the Hebrew Bible, written by the Children of Israel in the land of Israel.

Many other books were examined at this time, but they were not considered worthy to become part of the Bible. Many of them were included in the collection known as the Apocrypha. This is a Greek word which means "hidden." No doubt it was thought that these books would be hidden from the public, since they were not accepted as Holy Writ. This was not the result. The Apocrypha is a well-known collection, and some of its books give us much information about the life and times of the Jews of the Second Commonwealth.

After the final books became part of the Hebrew Bible, they were translated into other languages and accepted by Jews in other lands as sacred works. This is one way of showing how the Sanhedrin at Jabneh was considered the leading religious body not only by Palestinian Jewry but by the Jews of the world of that day.

The rabbis of this time were called "Tannaim" which means "students of the Law." Many, many stories have come down to us of their wit and wisdom. They were able to delve deeply into the mysteries of the Torah, and they were also able to hold their own in conversation with other outstanding men of the time.

Four leading Tannaim, Rabbis Gamaliel, Eleazar, Akiba, and Joshua, once visited Rome on a mission. They were received very well by the royal family, by Roman Jews, and by many Romans who were being converted to Judaism. Rabbi Joshua ben Chananya, who was very wise and learned in Jewish law, was also very quick and witty. He pitted his salty tongue against all who came.

Once the emperor said to Joshua, "I am better than Moses, for I am alive and he is dead."

The rabbi asked, "Can you command your subjects not to light fires for three days?"

"Of course," said the emperor, "I shall do so at once."

That night, the emperor and Joshua stood and watched from one of the palace windows. They saw smoke rising from a cottage in the distance.

"You see," said Rabbi Joshua, "your order which you gave today is not obeyed. But the command of Moses, which goes back fifteen hundred years, 'Thou shalt not light fires on the Sabbath day,' is still obeyed by Jews."

In a way, the years that Gamaliel II was patriarch could be

compared to the quiet years following Ezra and Nehemiah. It was a time of rebuilding land and homes. It was a period during which new ways of Jewish life developed which were handed down to future generations. It was an era when religious leaders were in the foreground.

Before long, a new religious leader would forsake the quiet of the Sanhedrin and its atmosphere of study and law. Instead, he would travel about the country gathering recruits for one last attempt to regain political independence for the Jews of Palestine. His name was Rabbi Akiba.

SOME QUESTIONS TO TALK OVER IN CLASS

Was the Sanhedrin in Jabneh a democratic body? Give examples to prove your answer.

Under which leaders were the Jewish people most successful—under the Maccabean kings, under Herod, under the men of the Sanhedrin in Jabneh? In answering this question, how did you measure "success"?

A PROJECT FOR THE CLASS

Every Jewish home should have a Bible, either in Hebrew or in an English translation. The standard Jewish translation is published by the Jewish Publication Society of America. Form a Bible Committee. Its purpose will be to get 100 per cent of the class to have a Bible at home. The committee can write to the Jewish Publication Society or to the Union of American Hebrew Congregations for information. Your teacher or your librarian will help.

READ

The Great March, Book I, by Lurie, "The Wicked Neighbor," p. 76.

Child's History of Jewish Life by Dorothy F. Zeligs, "A Parting Blessing," p. 45; "Rabbi Joshua ben Chananya," p. 46; "Rabbi Joshua and the Princess," p. 47; "The Lion and the Crane," p. 48.

The Sabbath Book by Abraham E. Millgram, "The Sabbath Taste," by Sadie R. Weilerstein, p. 105.

11. RABBI AND REBEL

RABBI AKIBA started out in life as a poor and ignorant shepherd. It is said he did not begin his studies until he was forty years old. In spite of his late start, he became one of the most learned, respected, and influential members of the Sanhedrin. He had hundreds of pupils. When he spoke in public, he led open discussions on questions of law and religion, and thousands of people came to listen.

Rabbi Akiba led the way to an important step. During the many years that had passed since the days of Hillel, thousands of decisions had been made on the meaning and interpretations of the laws of the Bible. These decisions became the Oral Law. Each rabbi had to study and remember what earlier rabbis had said about various laws. There was no orderly arrangement of these rulings.

Rabbi Akiba began such an orderly arrangement. He explained how one interpretation came from another, and how there might be more than one way of coming to a decision on a certain point. He arranged the laws in groups—the laws on marriage, the laws on the Sabbath, the laws on property. This was called Rabbi Akiba's "Mishnah" or "Teaching." Although it was not written down, Rabbi Akiba's Mishnah later became the basis for a written collection of the laws, which was simply called "The Mishnah." We shall learn about this enormously interesting and important collection later on. In the meantime, this temporary arrangement of the laws helped to clarify for rabbis and students the immense amount of material which had come into being since the days of the early Pharisees.

But Rabbi Akiba had another, very different role to play in Jewish history. For this student and teacher left the halls of teaching to lead another desperate war of rebellion against the Romans.

For almost fifty years, the Jews of Palestine had lived quietly under Rome. They always looked forward to the restoration of the Temple. The rabbis, for example, would discuss the duties of the priests in the Temple after it would be rebuilt. No one would ever admit the possibility that Jerusalem and the Temple were lost forever. Then a wonderful rumor began to be spread about the country. The emperor Trajan had promised to rebuild Jerusalem and the Temple! Hearts beat faster and exciting thoughts came to the minds of hopeful patriots. Trajan may have made such a promise to keep Palestine quiet.

Like many a Roman emperor, he sought new conquests. His first mark was the country of Parthia in Mesopotamia. Flushed with an early success, Trajan took over Adiabene, which held many converts to Judaism. Then he moved on, thinking to follow in the steps of Alexander the Great to world conquest. Trajan was not successful. All around him, his subject lands rose against him, and with them were the Jews in those lands. There was severe fighting in Egypt, in the Island of Cyprus, and the countries of Mesopotamia. The Jews were in the front ranks against the hated Romans. Thousands lost their lives.

Palestine took no part in these uprisings. Rome continued

its peaceful relations with the Jews. The patriarch and the emperor were on friendly terms. One of the emperors even reduced some of the harsh laws against the Jews.

A new emperor, named Hadrian, came on the throne of Rome. At first he too was very friendly to the Jews. He recalled to Rome a cruel governor. He released two Jews who had been condemned to death. Joshua ben Chananya had many discussions with the emperor when he visited Rome.

Hadrian also spoke about rebuilding Jerusalem. The people waited hopefully. At last Hadrian visited Palestine. One of his purposes was to see Jerusalem and to consider the problem of rebuilding it. He announced his plans. They were very different from those which filled the hearts of the Jews. Instead of the Temple of old, he prepared to erect a Temple to Jupiter, decorated with the head of a swine. Jerusalem was to be rebuilt as a pagan city, with the theaters, gymnasiums, and smaller pagan shrines found in such cities.

The hopes of the Jews were shattered. They might have submitted to new taxes. They might have compromised with a harsh governor. But this was too much. They were surrounded by foes. The old enmity of the Samaritans showed itself. The followers of Jesus, now known as Christians, had not taken part in the first war against Rome. Whenever possible they opposed the Jews. New harsh decrees came from the emperor. It seemed as if political independence—a break with Rome—would have to come.

Rabbi Akiba was in complete accord with this feeling. At eighty years, his heart still burned with youthful hopes and enthusiasm. He looked for a younger man to take to the field in actual battle.

He found Simon, a man of powerful strength and commanding appearance. He captured the imagination of Akiba.

He seemed like a second Judah Maccabee. Akiba renamed the young leader Bar Kochba, Son of a Star. Together they went around the country, recruiting men to fight with Bar Kochba.

Secretly preparations for war began. In caves and hiding places weapons were hidden away. Ambushes were prepared and fortresses secured. Roman war efforts were sabotaged. Smiths and makers of weapons for the Roman army fashioned weapons of weak and inferior metal, so that they would be useless if they were used against Jewish soldiers.

Hadrian's visit to Palestine took place during the years of 130 and 131. The building of the new Jerusalem began after he left. Disturbances broke out. Roman soldiers were ambushed. Cities were attacked.

Bar Kochba was an excellent commander. Young men from all over the country rallied to his side. Towns and villages fell one by one to the strong Jewish forces. Jerusalem was recaptured. Bar Kochba minted coins of his own as a sign of independence. On one side they said, "For the Deliverance of Jerusalem." For two years the Romans were blocked.

Hadrian realized that the reports from Palestine were serious. This was not a mere local uprising. Help was coming to the rebels from pagan lands nearby. Even the Samaritans had joined Bar Kochba. He commanded a large and dangerous fighting force.

Rome's most famous general, Julius Severus, was ordered to come from far-off Britain to take over the command of the war. Severus' strategy was slow and steady fighting. He did not hurry. He had the tremendous resources of the Roman Empire behind him. No matter how many soldiers he lost, more were sent to take their place. Unending supplies of food and weapons came to him through Syria. Time was on his side.

Severus did not meet Bar Kochba in open battle. Slowly, remorselessly, he fell on city after city. Bar Kochba led a magnificent struggle. For another year he pitted his strength against Severus.

Finally, in the year 135, at the fortress of Bethar, the two armies met. Bar Kochba was prepared for a final battle and a long siege. Severus made little headway. Then traitors showed him the way into the fortified city. The Romans entered. Bar Kochba's valiant men gave way at last to superior Roman forces. Bar Kochba was slain. His army was wiped out. The rebellion was quelled. All hopes of independence were completely lost.

The Romans were not content with a victory of arms. They

sought also a victory of the spirit. Hadrian realized that the core of Jewish strength was the religion of the Jewish people. For the first time, laws against religion and study were passed. Schools were closed. Teaching was forbidden. Observance of the Sabbath was not permitted. Teachers were hunted down for passing on to their pupils the lessons of the Torah. Rabbis were imprisoned for ordaining their pupils as rabbis. No Jew

could visit Jerusalem. Only on the 9th of Ov did they resist and bribe the guards to permit them to pray and weep at the Temple site. Rabbi Akiba was captured and put to death. He died as a martyr, reciting the words, "Sh'ma Yisroel, Adonoi Elohenu Adonoi Echod."

Many people were taken to Rome and sold as slaves. Many fled eastward to Babylonia, to join their brethren there and to begin what would become a glorious episode in Jewish history. The rest remained in Palestine, stubbornly holding on to their land and religion. In spite of harsh laws and rigorous decrees, they had no thought but to carry on life and law.

TALK OVER IN CLASS

Which could do more lasting harm to the Jews—Severus' victory over Bar Kochba, or Hadrian's laws against study and religion? Why?

How was the career of Rabbi Akiba an example of the idea of the Pharisees that learning should be the possession of every man? What other examples were there in the Sanhedrin?

READ

The Great March, Book I, by Lurie, "The Shepherd Rabbi," p. 80; "The Cock, the Donkey and the Candle," p. 88; "Fish Out of Water," p. 94.

Days and Ways by Gamoran, "They Showed the Way," p. 138.

Great Men in Israel by Weis, "Rachel and Akiba, the Shepherd," p. 31.

The World-Over Story Book edited by Norman Belth, "The Scholars' Holiday," by Ruth Sanders, p. 503.

Great Jewish Women by Levinger, "Rachel," p. 90.

Unit 4

The Big Change

History is like a great stage on which the nations of the world play their parts. As in the theater, these parts are acted against a background or setting. But the setting is not a painted canvas background; it is cities, regions, and countries in which men of many minds and varied thoughts live and mingle.

What would happen when Palestine was no longer the only setting for Jewish history? As Jews left the home of their fathers to live in different countries, the background of their lives changed. Could Jewish life go on, played against varied settings in new homes?

Over a period of hundreds of years, the stage was slowly prepared for a changing Jewish history in distant lands. Teachers and sages had to find a way for Jews to keep their beliefs and practices alive in any land where they might settle.

A movement for a new religion, based on Judaism, added to the drama of this period. World history took a new turn when the daughter religion, whose teachings came from Judaism, was accepted by millions of men. Judaism proved strong enough to pass its teachings on to others and also to hold on to its own followers.

The curtain rose on a new era.

With Their Treasures

12. OUTSIDE OF PALESTINE

BEFORE YOU read this chapter, look at the map on page 94. It tells a fascinating story of where Jews were living. Now we will find out how they got there and how they lived in their new homes.

Egypt, Assyria, Babylonia, Persia, Greece, Rome; they were in turn the conquering nations of the world. As they departed from the lands of their conquests, they took with them people from the countries they had subdued. Sometimes those whom they carried away as slaves began to influence the life of the master nation. This was the case when Greek slaves brought education to their Roman masters. Jewish captives also carried their beliefs and religion with them into their new environment.

How did Jews fare in the world outside of Palestine?

The year 721 B.C.E. records the first time when Jews left their land in large numbers. The Israelites were banished by the Assyrians. They were the Ten Lost Tribes, and we are not sure of what happened to them but it is believed that some of them founded Jewish settlements in Mesopotamia.

Judeans were brought to Babylonia with Nebuchadnezzar in 586 B.C.E. When the exiles returned to Judea, many Jews remained behind in Babylonia. We do not have many records of the early days of this settlement, but we know that there was always some contact with Judea. By the time Simon, the Maccabee, and his descendants ruled Palestine, this relationship became closer. Visitors from Babylonia made up a great portion of the pilgrims who came to Jerusalem for the festivals. The Babylonian Jews gave generously to the Temple. They wrote letters to the rabbis of Palestine. Messengers were sent regularly by the Sanhedrin to the cities of Babylonia to advise the Jews of the correct dates of the new moon and of the festivals. After the fall of the Temple in 70, and especially after the Bar Kochba revolt, Jews began to go to Babylonia from Palestine in increasing numbers. Babylonia became the home of a large Jewish community.

From the time of the Maccabean kings, Jews were found in the great cities and in the small towns along the seacoast of the Mediterranean. There were Jewish settlements all over the area known as Asia Minor. When the Roman emperor made the treaty with Simon he notified the heads of nineteen different lands where Jews probably lived even then. Some Jews had gone as far west as Spain and up to Gaul which is now France. Nearer home, in Syria, was the old Jewish settlement of Antioch, where thousands of Jews formed an important part of the city. The synagogue in Antioch was a magnificent building. One of the Syrian rulers gave back some vessels which had been taken from the Temple at the time of its destruction, and these were placed in the synagogue.

The largest group of Jews outside of Palestine was found in Egypt. Some scholars believe that about a million Jews lived in that land at the beginning of the Common Era.

The first Jews in Egypt were not traders or teachers. They were soldiers paid by the government for following this occupation. They served in a lonely outpost, called Elephantine. There they erected a temple, traded, built houses, and lived as equal citizens under the rule of Persia, which then held Egypt. When Egypt freed itself from Persian rule, the Jews left Elephantine for other places. Archeologists, working in Egypt between 1906 and 1908, found sheets of papyrus written in Aramaic hidden away for nearly twenty-five centuries. Among them were lists of names, business accounts, and letters to and from Jerusalem, which told about ancient Jewish Elephantine.

Alexander the Great built the seaport of Alexandria, where most of the Jews of Egypt lived. This city became one of the great trading centers of the world. Alexander brought Jews there with him. After his death, many more came to Alexandria. From then on, Jews began to mingle freely with the peoples of the world.

Most of Alexandria's huge Jewish population lived together in two parts of the city. They were governed by their own official, called the Ethnarch, who ruled almost as if they lived in an independent country. They took part in civic activities. They were merchants and traders. Some of them were important officials of the state. The office of the chief customs collector was twice filled by Jews. They adopted many Greek customs, spoke Greek for the most part, and in a number of outward ways acted like Greeks. Nevertheless, they considered themselves Jews, not Greeks.

The Jews of Alexandria gathered regularly for prayer on the Sabbath in their houses of worship and read the Torah there. Few Alexandrian Jews knew Hebrew. The Torah reading was therefore translated into Greek. They used the Septuagint, the Bible in Greek. They kept Jewish holidays and followed the Jewish calendar.

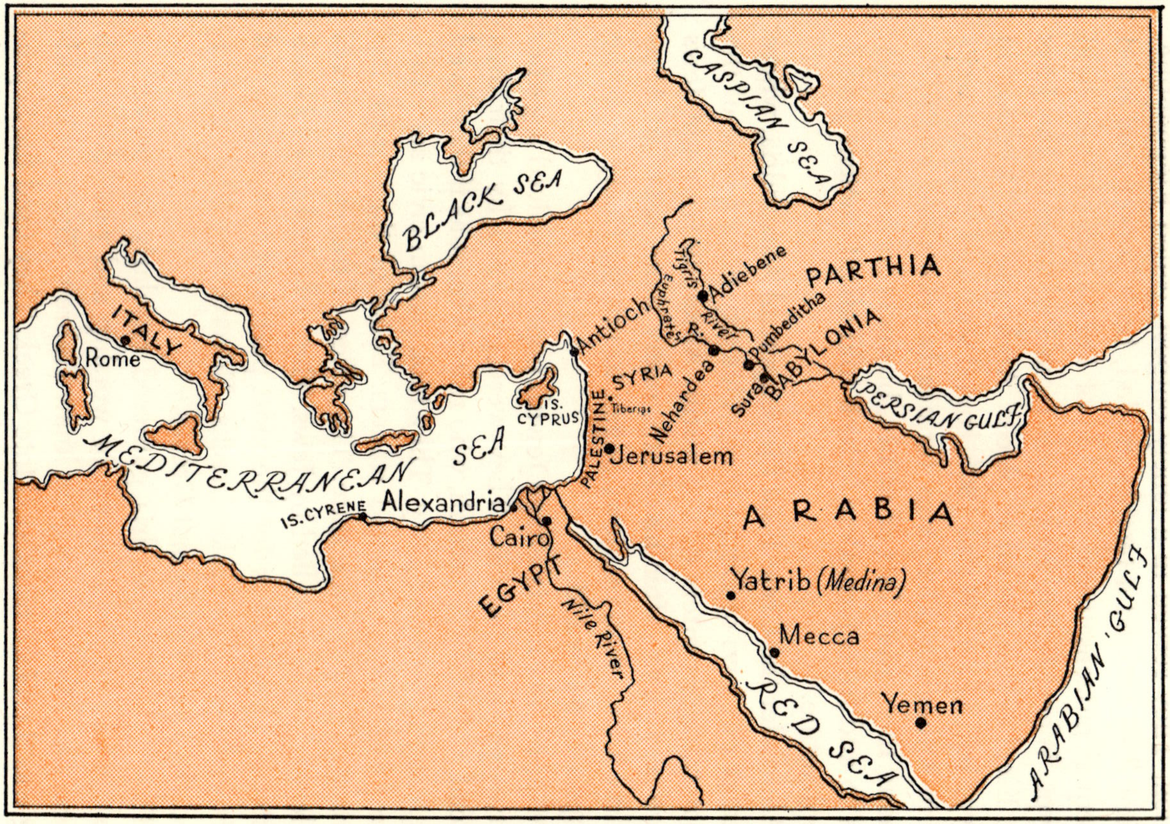

Where Jews Found New Homes

The Egyptian Jews were the only Jews outside of Jerusalem who had a temple of their own, with a High Priest and lesser priests. The temple stood in a town called Leontopolis, about two hundred miles south of Alexandria. It did not take the place of the Temple in Jerusalem. Alexandrian Jews faithfully paid their temple tax. They visited Jerusalem to celebrate the festivals in the Temple there. The temple at Leontopolis lasted a few years after the Temple in Jerusalem was destroyed. It was then closed by order of the Roman ruler.

Another large center of Jewish life outside of Palestine was the city of Rome. Some Jews lived in Rome as early as the days of Judah and Simon, the Maccabees. Then, when Pompey overcame Aristobulus in 63 B.C.E., he took the young ruler and his family with many other Jews captives to Rome. Most of the Jews became free men very soon. In Jerusalem, there was a synagogue called the "Synagogue of the Freedmen," which was probably organized when such Jews returned to Palestine. Another synagogue was called the "Synagogue of the Cyrenicians," for men who came from the Island of Cyrene, and one was known as the "Synagogue of the Alexandrians." These names are clues which tell us where Jews were living at that time.

Jewish merchants from Palestine, Egypt, and Asia Minor came to trade in Rome. It was the richest and most powerful community in the world, since it brought home wealth from all the countries it conquered. Money, grain, costly offerings, and slaves came into Rome as tribute.

After the close of the war with Rome, thousands of Jews were once more brought as captives to the land of the conqueror. Wherever Jews came as slaves, other Jews did their best to ransom them; that is, to pay for them and to set them free. In general, Jews did not make good slaves. In spite of their lowly position, they insisted on following their religion. It was inconvenient for a man to own slaves who would not work one day a week, and who would not eat the food that was set before them. The Romans probably set them free for very small sums.

Early in the first century, 20,000 Jews lived in Rome, along the banks of the Tiber River. Most of them were poor. Boats docked along the Tiber, and the Jews worked as laborers, transport workers, and boatmen. Some were shopkeepers and others were artisans. Years later, the bridge over the Tiber was called the Jews' Bridge.

Some wealthy Jews lived in other parts of the city. These were the members of the exiled royal family. Though they were prisoners, they maintained their kingly ways of living. It was the fashion to send members of the royal family from Judea to Rome. Herod's sons were educated in Rome and Agrippa spent his early life there, too.

Roman Jews kept close ties with Jerusalem. They paid their

Temple tax regularly. The Romans eyed the tax jealously. Once the emperor took for himself one hundred and twenty pounds of gold which had been collected for the Temple. As an excuse he declared that it was against Roman law to permit such a large sum of gold to leave the country.

The head of the synagogue was called the Archsynagogus. He was usually an educated man who could preach on the Sabbath. Other men had other duties. Some collected the taxes and funds for poor people and took care of the synagogue.

Special rules for the benefit of Jews were passed by the government. For example, no Jew was brought to court on the Sabbath. If grain was given out to the poor on Saturday, Jews were permitted to come for it on Sunday. Sometimes oil was furnished to the population. As Jews used only oil which was purified in their own special way, they received money instead of oil. To offset these privileges, extra taxes were levied against Jews.

One of the most interesting ways in which we have learned about Roman Jewry is through the discovery of Jewish catacombs. A catacomb is an underground burial place with long passages. The dead were buried in niches cut into the side walls of the passages, usually of rock. The first Jewish catacomb of Rome was discovered in 1602. Since then six catacombs have been found in Rome and others in different Italian cities and even in Africa. In Israel many such underground burial places had been discovered, though their arrangement is different from the Roman catacombs.

Jewish symbols cover the walls of the Roman catacombs. The esrog and the lulov, the seven-branched candlestick, and the shofor are among them. Passages from the Bible written most often in Greek, and sometimes in Latin, are over the tombs. Occasionally the Hebrew word שלום (sholom) is cut into the rock of the Roman catacombs.

So we see that even before the destruction of Jerusalem more Jews lived outside of Palestine than within it. They were found in many other places besides the great cities already mentioned. They were loyal to the countries in which they lived, but still looked to Palestine for leadership in their religious life. Roman, Greek, Syrian, Babylonian, and Palestinian Jews were held together by a bond of brotherhood. They all observed the same customs and were proud of the great ideals of their religion.

SOMETHING TO TALK OVER IN CLASS

Here are some laws and customs which were followed by Jews who lived in many different lands:

Studying the Bible	Learning the Hebrew language
Observing the festivals	Ransoming Jewish slaves
Using purified oil for the Sabbath	Reading the Torah on the Sabbath
Paying the Temple tax	Visiting Jerusalem

Which of these were done only by Jews of ancient times? Which are still carried on by Jews today?

A MAP ACTIVITY

Make an outline map from the map on page 94. Shade those areas which had a considerable Jewish population. Put in the important cities of the period.

READ

Great Jewish Women by Levinger, "Ima Shalom," p. 87.

Great Jews Since Bible Times by Elma E. Levinger, "The Wicked Emperor and the Good Philosopher," p. 14.

READINGS FOR TEACHERS

Unit 4 (*CHAPTERS 12–15*)

A History of the Jews, Book II, by Grayzel, Chap. I, pp. 201–209; Chap. II.

A History of the Jewish People by Margolis and Marx, Chaps. XXXIII–XXXV.

Jewish Post Biblical History by Bildersee, Chap. IV.

Studies in Judaism, 2nd Series, by S. Schechter, "A Hoard of Hebrew Manuscripts, I," p. 1; "A Hoard of Hebrew Manuscripts, II," p. 12.

History of the Jews in Rome by Hermann Vogelstein, Chaps. I, II.

The Jew in the Medieval World by Jacob R. Marcus, "Christianity Objects to the Sabbath," #20, p. 103.

13. FROM JUDAISM—A NEW RELIGION

ONE OF the first acts of any Jewish group when it came to a strange country was to form a synagogue. This did not always mean to erect a building. It meant to organize a congregation. Sometimes the congregants worshipped in the open. Sometimes they found a structure which was suitable for a synagogue. One man was appointed head of the synagogue. One of his duties was to choose for each week the man who read the Torah and the one who preached. These acts were not done by the same person every week. Those who were qualified took turns. Another official took charge of the Temple tax. He collected it and sent it on to Jerusalem.

The language of most of the world at that time was Greek. Even in Rome, the educated people preferred Greek to Latin. Jews outside of Palestine spoke Greek. In fact, Hebrew as a spoken tongue had largely given way to Aramaic even in Palestine. Hebrew was the language of prayer, of the learned men, and of legal discussions. Letters regarding the Torah and the Oral Law were written in Hebrew. In the synagogue in Palestine the Bible was read in Hebrew and translated into Aramaic.

The Septuagint or Greek translation of the Bible had a twofold purpose. One was to bring the Bible to those Jews who knew only Greek. The other was to bring the Bible to the non-Jewish world. Thus the men of other nations became acquainted with the wisdom, poetry, and religious ideas which are found in the Bible.

Many other Jewish books were known by non-Jews as well as Jews. Through them the knowledge of Judaism was spread. You know that some of these books are now in the Apocrypha. Among them are some which have come down to us only in Greek, although they were probably written originally in Hebrew.

At times important discoveries of such books are made by chance. In 1896, part of an original Hebrew manuscript came to light in a strange way. In that year, two English ladies traveling in Cairo, bought some fragments of an ancient Hebrew scroll. They brought them back to Cambridge University in England, and gave them to a great Jewish scholar, Dr. Solomon Schechter. Dr. Schechter made a surprising discovery. One of these bits of parchment turned out to be part of a Hebrew book called, *The Wisdom of Ben Sira.* Up to this time, only Greek translations of "Ben Sira" had ever been seen by scholars. Dr. Schechter set off on an adventurous search to Cairo. He was seeking more of these ancient leaves of parchment. He found many of them in the dusty attic of an old synagogue. To this day, they have not all been completely studied. Who can tell what important information still lies hidden in their faint, hard-to-read characters? One of you boys or girls who is reading this history may some day become a great Jewish scholar and give their contents to the world.

Alexandria was a city of culture and learning. Many Egyptian Jews were pupils of Greek teachers of science, philosophy, and art. The most famous Greek-Jewish philosopher was named Philo. Philo was a member of an aristocratic family of Alexandrian Jews. He knew the works of Greek thinkers and Jewish scholars. He wrote many books and essays. In these writings he tried to bring together Hebrew and Greek knowledge and wisdom.

Philo described for the non-Jew the laws of Moses found in the Bible. He explained their excellence and importance for good living. For his Jewish readers he tried to show how Greek thought could be added to and combined with Jewish ideas. His works were known to educated men in all centers of knowledge and study.

Philo's knowledge of Greek lore did not make him unfaithful to the religion of his fathers. He remained a steadfast Jew.

Educated Romans also became acquainted with the Septuagint and with books written by Jews about their people and their religion. Josephus wrote four books. In them, he told the history of his people and defended their ideas against Roman writers. His purpose was to show what a wonderful people the Jews were, even though they had lost the war to the Romans.

The world before and after the first century of the Common Era was a pagan world. That is, most of the people prayed to many gods. Statues of the gods were found in every city. Festivals which honored different gods were celebrated. Each of the gods had certain special qualities. One was worshipped for power, one for beauty, and one for wisdom.

At once you can see the first great difference between Judaism and paganism. Judaism taught that there is only one God. "The Lord is One, and His Name is One."

The other important difference is found in what religion means to a man and how it influences his life.

The prophets declared that saying prayers and bringing a sacrifice did not bring out the real meaning of religion. Belief in Judaism and the love of God meant acting honestly and justly and being charitable to those in need. An evil deed could not be wiped out by a sacrifice.

Pagan religions made no connections between a man's conduct and his worship of the gods. In the stories told about the gods, their own conduct was often not an example to follow. Paganism did not try to teach a man how to behave toward his family, his friends, and his neighbors. Although the Greeks and the Romans had great artists and sculptors, fine poets and splendid thinkers, they had not advanced in their religion. They were still pagans.

The religion of the ancient gods was controlled by the government. It was the duty of a Roman citizen to observe the festivals and sacrifices to the gods. Even Jews had to pay a tax to the Temple of Jupiter, although they had special rights to observe their own religion.

As the knowledge of Judaism spread in the settlements where Jews had come to live, many pagans became dissatisfied with their religion. They came to a point where the ancient worship of many gods no longer satisfied them. They could not accept the idea of gods in the form of men or animals. Stories of gods and goddesses living like people seemed foolish. They looked for a religion which had a basis in righteousness and which could help them live a good and happy life.

The ideas of Judaism attracted them. Jewish family life and customs seemed good to them. The day of rest was pleasant and welcome. They wished to follow the teachings of the prophets.

Some non-Jews began to follow Jewish customs. They did not call themselves Jews, but they believed in one God. They observed the Sabbath, and they did not eat the meat of swine.

Many pagans went further. They were converted to Judaism. They were not the first converts. You remember how Queen Helena and King Izates and members of their court at Adiebene became Jews. One high-born Roman named Aquilla who may have been related to the emperor was converted to Judaism. He is said to have been a pupil of Rabbi Akiba. Later on, this converted Jew made a new and learned translation of the Bible into Greek. Aquilla's Bible is known for the exact way in which he translated every Hebrew word. He examined each letter and each syllable before he decided on a translation. He corrected many errors which had been allowed to creep into the Septuagint.

As more and more people became converts to Judaism, laws against conversion were passed in Rome. It became a crime against the state. One Roman noble named Flavius was a nephew of the emperor. Because he defied the law and was converted to Judaism, he was executed. A short time later, the emperor was killed. Flavius had been in line for the throne. Thus, only a thin thread of circumstance prevented a Jew from becoming the emperor of Rome.

Besides those who actually became Jews, a great many more men and women were interested in the ideas of Judaism, but were not ready to take on the strict observance of Jewish law. Jews believed that observing the Law was a way of showing their love of God. They found joy in following out the rules and observances of the Torah. They were happy to keep the holidays and festivals and to pray at the appointed times. They did not find these laws hard to keep. Newcomers to Judaism, however, did not look at Jewish law in this way. To many of them the laws of the Torah were a burden.

In the early days of the first century a man named Saul appeared who gathered together the thousands of people who were ready to cast off paganism. He brought them a new religion. It was named Christianity to show its allegiance to Jesus whom they called Christ, anointed one. It took over the ideas of one God, of righteousness, and of mercy which were taught in the Bible. But in place of the Torah, the Law, it demanded faith in Jesus.

Saul was a Jew who was born in Tarsus, Cilicia, north of Syria. He studied with the rabbis in Jerusalem. At first he was a strict Pharisee. Later he became a Christian, believing that Jesus was the Messiah.

Saul began a life of traveling. His purpose was to make converts for Christianity. He visited almost all the countries which were under Roman rule. His first visits were to the places where Jews were living. When he came to a city he went immediately to the synagogue where Jews gathered. There he spoke of the glories of Judaism, but he always added his belief in Jesus as the Messiah. He declared that only through belief in Jesus could a man be saved and have peace in the world to come.

The Jews could not accept Saul's statement that he spoke for the Messiah. He was often expelled from the synagogue. After a while he went directly to non-Jews, pagans who were ready to accept some of the basic ideas of Judaism. These ideas were not new to them. They had heard of them from their neighbors, the Jews.

The Hebrew name, Saul, was changed to the Greek name, Paul. For thirty years Paul continued his travels and his work. Thousands of people became converts to the new religion.

Many of the early Christians considered themselves Jews—Jews who believed in Jesus. That is the way the first followers of Jesus in Palestine thought of themselves. Paul himself always managed to return to Jerusalem in time for feast days and holidays. However, they were in truth no longer Jews. They did not observe all Jewish law. They were the first followers of a new religion.

Because of the rules against conversion, the early Christians in Rome often suffered for their faith. For the world was still more pagan than Christian, more pagan than Jewish. Gradually, Christians became more numerous. The turning point came at about the year 325 when the emperor Constantine was converted to Christianity. It became a powerful state religion which spread over land and sea. The officials of the church, the priests, bishops, and later the popes, exerted a tremendous influence over kings and emperors.

The Roman Empire grew weaker and was divided between East and West. It could not recover its former greatness. The world was no longer under the rule of one strong empire. Instead, Christianity united people and nations. Of course

this did not happen quickly. It took more than three centuries.

Christian leaders often lost sight of the fact that the founders of their religion were Jews, and that its main ideas came from Judaism. Later on, new customs were added and changes were made in Christianity which emphasized its differences from Judaism. For example, Sunday became the day of rest instead of Saturday. At first the Christian church used the Jewish calendar; later on a calendar of its own was developed.

In Palestine, in the Roman Empire, and in Babylonia, the Jews saw the rise of Christianity. They ceased to look for converts. The main stream of Judaism continued its course. The rabbis centered their efforts on teaching. They spread the knowledge of the Torah among their own people. They strengthened their faith in God and in the worth of their own religion.

In the years that Christianity rose and grew strong, surprising events were taking place in Palestine. Splendid leaders gave it new strength and helped Palestine hold on to its place as the center of Jewish life. Once again, we turn our attention to the Jews of Palestine.

TALK OVER IN CLASS

What attracted pagans to Judaism?

What did they find in Christianity that came from Judaism?

Why did so many of them choose Christianity instead?

Should the Jews of Palestine have sent out a missionary to try to get converts?

Are there converts to Judaism today?

14. THE TEACHERS IN GALILEE

THE JEWS of Palestine were a small group living in the midst of larger surrounding Jewish settlements. At first it seemed almost impossible for them to recover after Bar Kochba's defeat. Judea never did become a thriving community again. Great areas had been laid waste by soldiers who marched over fields and farms. Villages and towns were destroyed. Jerusalem was inhabited by Syrian and Phoenician soldiers. Jews lived only in a few cities along the coast.

Rome laid a heavy hand on the people and the land. New and greater taxes were imposed. Study and teaching were absolutely forbidden. All schools were closed. No rabbis could be ordained. Teachers met pupils secretly and in hidden places. Sabbath observance, circumcision, and following Jewish law could be punished by death.

A grave problem arose. Many people were ready to die for the sake of the Torah. Should men give up their lives to defy the Roman laws?

In an attic in Lydda a group of teachers secretly gathered. They asked themselves, "Is it more important to save our people's lives or to observe Jewish law?" The answer came after trying days and nights of discussion. Life must go on. The people must accept Roman edicts. There were only three things they were not permitted to do: They could not worship idols. They had to be faithful to their husbands and wives, so Jewish family life would continue. They could not shed innocent blood.

For about five years the harsh laws of religious persecution held sway. Then they were repealed by a more kindly Roman emperor. Only one edict was kept—Jews were not permitted to return to Jerusalem. The Romans were still severe masters. Crushing taxes continued. But the Jews were ready to accept these burdens in return for religious freedom.

Fortunately, Galilee was fairly prosperous. Its cities had not been affected by the Bar Kochba rebellion. It still had thriving farms, well-fed flocks, and going industries. From the shattered towns of Judea, many people fled northward. In Galilee they found new homes and the opportunity to engage in farming, fishing, and crafts.

The center of religious life moved to the town of Usha in

Galilee. Scholars from various parts of the country came together there. One rabbi named Simon ben Yochai came out of the cave where he had been hiding for thirteen years. He had been forced to live there because he had spoken forcefully against the Romans. Seven pupils of Rabbi Akiba who had fled to Babylonia returned to Palestine to carry on their master's work. Akiba's most brilliant young follower, Rabbi Meir, became one of the leaders of the group. The scholars sent out a proclamation: "Anyone who has studied, come and teach. Anyone who has not studied, come and learn." Simon II, the son of Gamaliel II, was named Patriarch.

Rabbi Meir was an unusual person. He was a scribe, a copier of sacred books, a writer of scrolls of the Law. To copy a book of the Bible is not an easy task. Not a word, not even the stroke of a letter, may be different from the traditional copy. Rabbi Meir had an exceptional memory. Once he came to a small town on the eve of Purim. There was no Megillah or Scroll of Esther in the whole town. In spite of this, the congregation was able to hold a Purim service. Rabbi Meir recited the entire Book of Esther by heart for the assembled townspeople. With such a memory, he continued the task which Rabbi Akiba had begun of arranging the many laws and decisions of the Oral Law in orderly divisions.

Rabbi Meir had a lighter side too. He liked to tell and write fables. He wrote more than three hundred fables about the sly, wise, and cunning fox.

Rabbi Meir's wife, Beruriah, was one of the few women who is remembered as a scholar and a teacher. She, too, had her pupils. A saying of hers, "Look to the end of the matter," was accepted as a principle of study. It meant to carry through and not to come to a decision until all sides of a question had been investigated.

Some of Rabbi Meir's sayings are well known. He said, "When thou art in Rome, do as the Romans do." He also declared, "Better few prayers with devotion, than many without it."

The rabbis, scholars, and teachers who gathered in Usha found an extraordinary leader when Simon's son, Judah, became Patriarch in the year 170. He held the office until his death in 217—almost fifty years. Judah combined in one person many qualities of leadership. He was striking in appearance, firm in his decisions, learned in the Law, and a brilliant teacher. At a time when Palestine was considered one of the most lowly of Roman provinces, he was called Prince. He was treated as a prince by Roman emperors and governors. To this day he is called Judah ha-Nasi, or Judah the Prince. He was also called "Rabbi," not Rabbi Judah. Everyone knew that "Rabbi" meant Judah ha-Nasi. He brought honor to the title "Rabbi." His home was a place of culture and wisdom. He was eager to bring Hebrew back as a spoken language, and Hebrew was used in his home. Some people said his servants spoke better Hebrew than some of the scholars who used Hebrew only for reading and writing.

Judah had great wealth. He lived in a fine home, first in Sepphoris and later in Tiberias. He assisted poor students. During a time of famine he also distributed grain to all who needed it. He kept in mind the needs of the people. One of the problems of the day was how to pay the taxes demanded by the Romans. According to Jewish law, the land was supposed to lie fallow, that is, to rest, every seventh year. It was called the Sabbatical Year. When Palestine was under Jewish rule, taxes were not collected during the seventh year. But the Romans came for taxes year in and year out. They paid no attention to the Sabbatical Year. This problem came before

"Rabbi" and the rabbis who met with him. Under Judah's leadership, they decided to permit the farmers to raise enough grain during the seventh year to pay the taxes.

Judah ha-Nasi also had his faults. Perhaps some of his qualities were responsible for these faults. Because he was accustomed to wealth and power, he was proud and haughty. He did not permit the democratic ways of the Sanhedrin of Jabneh to be followed. He did not allow anyone but himself to ordain rabbis. He refused to ordain certain teachers because they had boldly opposed him. Even in lands outside of Palestine he appointed judges and teachers. All the powers of the Sanhedrin were transferred to him.

There may have been reasons for Judah's insistence on keeping power in his own hands. Palestine was no longer the home of the great mass of the Jewish people. Christians and non-Jews of many foreign countries outnumbered the Jews. Neither were the Jews wealthy nor politically strong. But Palestine was still the center of Jewish religious life. Judah's purpose may have been good—to retain the position of Palestine as the sacred land—but his methods often met with discontent.

Judah ha-Nasi is remembered, mainly, for one magnificent accomplishment. He finally arranged the entire Oral Law into one great collection. Like Rabbi Akiba and Rabbi Meir, Judah prepared a Mishnah, or "Teaching," as a textbook for his pupils. Gradually, it became more than this. Over a long period of years, he and his pupils went through hundreds of discussions and decisions on the Bible and its laws, which had been accumulating for almost six hundred years. They began with the time of Hillel and went up to their own day. The work of one hundred and forty-eight Tannaim were included in the collection. All the opinions on one matter were placed under one heading. All subjects which were connected with each other were brought together.

The great work of Judah ha-Nasi was called the Mishnah. No other book was known by that name after his day. His collection took the place of the works prepared by earlier rabbis.

The Mishnah governed Jewish life for many long years. Jewish scholars spent a great part of their life studying it. We shall try to learn just a little about the Mishnah in the next chapter.

SOMETHING TO TALK OVER IN CLASS

How were Judah ha-Nasi and Hillel similar? How were they different?

PUT YOURSELF IN HIS PLACE

Select five or more members of the class. Each one is to take the part of a well-known rabbi. Give each one a chance to act or say something to show which rabbi he is trying to be. The rest of the class will try to guess who he is.

READ

The Great March, Book I, by Lurie, "The Guardians of the Torah," p. 99.

Great Jews Since Bible Times by Levinger, "The Rabbi and the Emperor," p. 36.

Watchmen of the Night by Kalisher, "Food for All," p. 21.

Great Jewish Women by Levinger, "Beruria," p. 87; "The Wife of Sidon," p. 101.

15. THE MISHNAH

TRY TO think of the laws and rules you obey every day. You go to school. You watch the red and green lights when you cross the street. If you need something you buy it and pay for it. You obey laws of health, like keeping clean and washing an apple before you eat it. If you play a game of basketball, you follow the rules of the game. You stop when the referee blows his whistle.

So you see, your life is governed by law. Some of the laws are written down and are enforced by the government. You obey others because you know they help you and your family, your city and your country.

If you were arranging the laws you live by, you would probably start out by making a list of things you do. Then you would arrange them under different headings. These headings might be, School, Sports, Home, and Religion.

The rabbis who prepared the Mishnah with Judah ha-Nasi did this very thing. First they examined the laws, thousands of them, which had come into being in order to explain the Bible. Then they put them all down under separate headings.

The Mishnah is divided into six parts. Their names are, "Seeds," "Feasts," "Women," "Damages," "Holy Things," and "Laws of Purity." *Seeds* deals mainly with agricultural matters and *Feasts* with the Sabbath, festivals, and holidays.

Women contains laws about marriage and divorce. *Damages* is the code of civil and criminal laws. Sacrifices and Temple worship were considered in *Holy Things. Laws of Purity* is concerned with rules observed by the Levites and also tells of many rules of hygiene for the welfare of men and women.

The Mishnah is written in short Hebrew sentences, though many Aramaic and Greek words are found in it. The language of the Mishnah has served as a model of good Hebrew. Those men who studied the Bible and the Mishnah and knew them well became masters of the Hebrew language.

The Hebrew word for law is "Halachah." The Mishnah consists mainly of Halachah. Occasionally, a story or a wise saying of a rabbi is also included. Such writings: legends, stories, history, are called "Agaddah." You will learn more about Agaddah later on.

Attached to one of the divisions of the Mishnah is a short book called *Pirkei Ovos,* the *Sayings of the Fathers. Pirkei Ovos* has only five chapters, but in these few pages are gathered many of the wonderful teachings of the rabbis, which had to do with honest living and right thinking. The wise and witty words of Jochanan ben Zakkai, of Joshua ben Chananya, of Rabbi Akiba, and of Rabbi Meir are found in *Pirkei Ovos.* A host of other teachers and their pupils are quoted.

Here are a few examples of the Sayings of the Fathers. Rabbi Simeon the Righteous said, "The world is based on three things: on Torah, on worship, and on the practice of charity."

Rabbi Eleazar ben Azariah said, "One whose wisdom exceeds his deeds—unto what can he be compared? Unto a tree whose branches are many and the roots few, so that when the wind comes, it uproots it and overturns it. But one whose deeds exceed his wisdom—unto what can he be compared? Unto a tree whose branches are few and the roots many, so that even if all the winds in the world come and blow upon it, they shall not move it out of its place."

Rabbi Judah ben Tema said, "Be bold as a leopard, and swift as an eagle, and fleet as a hart, and strong as a lion, to do the will of thy Father who is in heaven."

The rabbis were fond of making a chain of sentences, one linked to another. For example, Ben Zoma said, "Who is wise? He who learns from all men. Who is mighty? He who overcomes his temper. Who is rich? He who is satisfied with his position in life. Who is honored? He who honors others."

These are only a few quotations from *Pirkei Ovos*. It is full of good advice and wise sayings.

It was the custom to read and study the *Pirkei Ovos* in the synagogue, chapter by chapter, on the Sabbaths between Passover and Shovuos. This study continued throughout the summer. In many temples and synagogues this custom is still continued either in Hebrew or with an English translation. In this way, those who are not scholars of the Mishnah can enjoy the instruction of the sages of long ago.

The completion of the Mishnah did not mean that learning and study came to an end. Now students had the Mishnah as well as the Bible to study and consider.

In addition, they were busy with another collection of writings called the Midrash. Midrash comes from the word "lidrosh" which means "to seek." The Midrash does seek the religious meaning of the Bible. Such explanations go back to the days of Ezra, the Scribe.

The Midrash explains the Bible not according to its laws but in a simpler way. It appeals to men's feelings and their hearts. It consists of ancient legends and stories, fables and proverbs, and retells many of the Bible stories. Details not given in the Bible are imagined to make the story more lively and more colorful. It is written for the ordinary reader, not for the scholar or teacher. Its purpose is to advise a man how to act toward his fellow man, and how to comfort him in time of need. However, the collections of the Midrash have been used and are used today by rabbis and speakers, in sermons and talks, for they are filled with charm, and delight the listener as well as the reader.

Volumes of Midrash have been written about the various books of the Bible and about the holidays and festivals. They continued to be written and collected for many years.

Slowly the number of Jews in Palestine became smaller. The break between Jews and Christians had long since taken place. Christians now made holy pilgrimages to Palestine. Helen, the mother of Emperor Constantine, who first proclaimed Rome to be a Christian country, came to Palestine. She declared that she had discovered the very cross on which Jesus was crucified, and the site of his tomb. On this site, a large church was erected. From that time forth, many churches were built all over Palestine. Strange to say, even though most Christians were not friendly to Jews, some Christian scholars came to Palestine to study with rabbis and teachers.

Laws against Jews in Palestine and in other parts of the Roman Empire became harsher. The building of new synagogues was forbidden. No Jew could have a Christian slave. In spite of opposition, non-Jews accepted Judaism and so more laws against conversion to Judaism were passed. Another unsuccessful uprising against Rome took place in Palestine. The Jews had to flee from Galilee. Tiberias, Sepphoris and Lydda were almost deserted.

It became difficult even to hold meetings of the Sanhedrin. Its work was interrupted. The Patriarch, Hillel II, came to an important decision. In the year 360, he sent a message to all the heads of the communities of Jews outside of Palestine. He told them how the calendar was fixed. He gave them the rules for deciding on the new months and on the dates of the festivals. He explained the important rules for deciding on a leap year.

From the earliest days of the Sanhedrin, it had held authority over the calendar. The patriarch was the head of the Sanhedrin. When Hillel the Patriarch sent his messengers outside of Palestine with the rules for the calendar and the leap year, he knew what it meant. He was giving up one of the most important duties of his office. He gave up the place which Palestine had always had as the seat of final authority for the whole of Jewry.

Hillel II felt that the welfare of his people in other parts of the world was most important. The time might come when it would become impossible to fix the calendar in Palestine. Messengers might not be allowed to leave the country. He made sure that Jews all over the world would have one calendar, and would celebrate their festivals and holy days at the same time.

In 361, an emperor named Julian came to the throne of Rome. He was a new-found friend. He promised to repeal the harsh laws against the Jews and to help them rebuild the Temple. He sent a letter of friendship to the patriarch. But

Julian's promise was never redeemed. He died after he had reigned only two years. In church history, Julian is called the "Apostate," which means one who has forsaken his religion.

The period of intense Jewish life in Palestine was coming to a close. For another fifty years, a patriarch continued to rule. In 425, the Patriarch Gamaliel VI died. He left no son to carry on. The emperor decided to abolish the office.

The title of Patriarch began with Gamaliel II, in 80, and continued through his descendants for fifteen times in succession. For about three hundred and fifty years, the Jews of Palestine were ruled by the members of one family. The patriarchs were also the leaders of the Jews of the rest of the world. In these years, the Jews of Palestine showed that they could overcome the burdens imposed on them by harsh rulers. They continued to create in the fields of religion, education, and law. They were the spiritual leaders of the Jews of the world.

Not every patriarch was of the same high caliber as Gamaliel II and Judah ha-Nasi. Nevertheless, it was good to have a ruler who could deal with Rome when necessary, and who regulated Jewish affairs. Many of the patriarchs, even those who served at the close of this period, were held in high esteem by the Roman rulers. Because of this, the life of the people was sometimes made easier by favors granted by the emperor.

By this time, the majority of the Jews had left their homeland. Most of them had moved to Babylonia. But some settlements remained in Palestine. They became active again about 200 years later. Palestine was never without Jews, and pilgrims always found some of their brethren when they visited the land of their fathers.

The treasures of Judaism which came from Palestine—the Bible, the Mishnah, and the teachings of the rabbis—were transplanted to other lands. Without them, there would have

been no Jewish life outside of Palestine. The scattered Jewish people continued because a foundation of religion and law had been laid by the Jews of Palestine. We might say that the first patriarchs, Abraham, Isaac, and Jacob, began this work and it continued until the days of the last patriarchs, the house of Hillel.

But by the year 400, the future of the Jewish people had already shifted to a new center, Babylonia.

SOMETHING TO DO

Write a short composition about the Mishnah. Describe what it is, how it is divided, and the names of some rabbis who helped to prepare it.

TALK OVER IN CLASS

What did fixing the calendar mean to the patriarch?

READINGS FOR TEACHERS

The Bar Mitzvah Treasury edited by Azriel Eisenberg, "Torah the Best Merchandise" (from the Midrash), taken from *The Ma-Aseh Book,* Vol. I, by Moses Gaster.

Unit 5

A Center of Learning

What a contrast the quiet life of the Jewish community in Babylonia was to the unsettled situation in Palestine! Young men of Babylonia who had studied under Judah ha-Nasi, returned to their native land. Instead of a harsh government, they found kindly rulers. Instead of the hum of busy schools, they found learning almost neglected.

Here was a challenge. The spark of the Torah had to be kindled. Jewish life in Babylonia had stood still too long.

A remarkable story is about to unfold before us.

A Scene in Babylonia

16. THE JEWS OF BABYLONIA

AT FIRST, Babylonia was something to joke about. "Why do the Babylonians have round heads?" a man asked Hillel. He was trying to win a bet by making Hillel angry. (Hillel did not become angry. He gave a sensible answer, and the man lost his bet.)

During the years that the Temple stood, Palestinian Jews did not think very highly of the Jews of Babylonia. It is true that thousands of Babylonian Jews visited Jerusalem during the pilgrim festivals. Babylonian Jews collected a huge sum yearly for the Temple tax. Students came from Babylonia to study at the schools and academies in Palestine. But the pride of the Jews was Jerusalem. The center of Judaism was Palestine. Even after the Temple fell, Palestine held its position of leadership in the Jewish world for many years. Students from Babylonia came to the schools at Jabneh and then to Usha and Tiberias.

By the time Judah ha-Nasi was patriarch, the Babylonian Jews were beginning to count in the Jewish world. For almost seven hundred years, from the time of exile in 586 B.C.E., they had lived in the land of the two rivers. These were the Tigris and the Euphrates, the very rivers which Abraham crossed in his wanderings from Mesopotamia to Canaan. Slowly but surely, Babylonia began to outshine Palestine in numbers, in wealth, and even in scholarship.

There were many reasons for this situation. Babylonian Jews did not suffer the turmoil and troubles of the Jews of Palestine. They were under the rule of the Parthian Empire. This part of the world was independent of Rome and its territories. Rome cast envious eyes on this rich and inviting land. She tried without success to take it over.

At the same time, the position of Jews under Roman rule was growing more difficult. Not only Palestine, but the settlements in Egypt and in Italy and in Asia Minor were growing weaker under harsh Roman laws.

After the year 70 and especially after the failure of the Bar Kochba rebellion, many Palestinians fled to Babylonia. Later, a few of them returned to Palestine. Some came back to study and to carry on the work of their teachers. Others rejoined their families.

Many, many remained in Babylonia. They founded large cities where nearly all the inhabitants were Jews. During the years when wars had passed them by, the Babylonian Jews had grown into a strong and wealthy community.

Babylonia was like a great garden. Palm trees grew everywhere. Vast farms of grain, wheat, fruit, and vegetables were found all over. Large herds of cattle grazed contentedly.

Among the large landowners and farmers were a number of Jews. Some Jews rented farms from their more wealthy neighbors. They paid their rent in labor and produce. These farmers were poorer folk, but life for them was still comfortable and pleasant.

In the cities, Jews were traders and shopkeepers. Others were laborers who worked on the famous "canals" which

watered the soil. They dug the canals and kept them clean. When the writer of Psalm 137 wrote about the "Waters of Babylon," he meant streams, rivers, and also canals. Jews did practically every kind of work. In one book, we read that they even made very good beer.

The two rivers wound their way south toward the Persian Gulf. Along their banks great cities rose. One of them was named Nehardea. Only Jews lived in this city. It was to this city that the Jews of Babylonia sent their Temple tax. It went from Nehardea to Jerusalem in a well-guarded caravan.

The Jewish settlement of Babylonia was almost independent. It was autonomous, that is, it was governed by its own ruler under the Persian king. The head of the Jewish community was called the Prince of the Exile. This name tells a story.

The Prince of the Exile traced his family back to King Jehoiachin. This is the king who was taken captive to Babylonia by Nebuchadnezzar. He was freed after some years and lived in princely style at the court of the Persian king. King Jehoiachin was a descendant of King David. In this way, the Jews of Babylonia were still governed by a ruler of the House of David.

Another name for the Prince of the Exile was the Exilarch. The Persian king usually held the exilarch in high esteem. In rank, the exilarch was fourth from the king. Under him the Jews lived as though they were in their own country.

The exilarch reminds us of King Solomon, rather than King David. He usually lived on a great and beautiful estate with many servants and slaves. When he went out, runners ran ahead, announcing him and clearing the way, as though he were the monarch of the land.

The exilarch collected the taxes from the people for the king. Part of the taxes collected were kept by him, and he became very wealthy. There was a curious rule about the collection of taxes. Scholars did not have to pay any taxes. No doubt this rule was meant to help poor men who wished to study. It sometimes worked a hardship on other people. Some scholars became very wealthy. In spite of their wealth, they paid no taxes. On the other hand, other people continued to pay their share of the taxes, to support the country, the king, and the exilarch.

The exilarch appointed judges. Jewish law was followed in the courts. The only time a Jew went to a Persian court was when a dispute came up with a Persian. All other questions were solved by Jewish judges, according to Jewish law. The final judge was the exilarch.

The exilarchs were not usually men of learning, like Judah ha-Nasi, who was ruler, teacher, and rabbi. Most of them respected the rabbis and teachers. Sons and daughters of the families of the exilarchs and of the great teachers often married each other.

One important fact stands out in the history of the Babylonian Jewish settlement. With all its wealth and prosperity, it did not take on a position of importance in the Jewish world for many centuries. It had to wait until it had teachers and rabbis to take their places with the exilarch and his officers.

Shortly before the year 200, some of the young students who had been studying in Galilee with Judah ha-Nasi and the great Tannaim, returned to Babylonia. They were eager to bring to their country the knowledge that they had been given in Palestine. The best known of these early teachers are named Rav and Samuel.

Rav's real name was Abba. He also had a nickname, Aricho, "the tall one." As he became well known, his real name was forgotten. He was given the title of greatest respect, "Rav," Master or Teacher, just as Judah was called "Rabbi" in Palestine.

Rav began his career in a very ordinary way. The exilarch appointed him inspector of markets. To do his work well, it was necessary to travel around the country. Rav was very unhappy to see that his countrymen did not know Jewish tradition and did not study the Torah. He determined to do something about it.

He opened a school in the southern part of Babylonia in a city called Sura, on the shores of Lake Sura. It was not long before the school became famous. Students came to Sura from all over the land.

Rav did not want to teach only men who wished to become teachers and scholars. He wanted as many people as possible to know the Torah, the Mishnah, and the wisdom of other Jewish writings. A brand new method of teaching was begun by Rav.

Twice a year, a month was set aside for study. One month was Ador, at the beginning of the spring. The other was Elul, when autumn came. At these times, thousands of men left their homes, their farms, and their business and came to Sura. For a month at a time, from early morning until the evening, they studied. They listened to lectures by Rav and by the teachers he had gathered at Sura.

This was not all. The week before the important festivals was also set aside for study. During these weeks, even more people came to Sura. There were not enough houses to give shelter to everyone. Many visitors slept in the open, on the banks of the lake. These visits to Sura remind us of the holiday visits to Jerusalem before the year 70.

The exilarch would come to Sura, too. He would arrive in his carriage, dressed in his princely garments and surrounded by his courtiers. The people waited for a glimpse of their ruler.

At such a time, Sura was the meeting place of the two leaders of the Jews of Babylonia. They were the Prince of the Exile who stood for royalty and power, and the head of the school, the symbol of knowledge and faith.

These gatherings were called the Kallah, and the months were Kallah months. During these months, the courts did not hold sessions. All life was directed toward study. In Babylonia, no man could say he could not study.

Rav interested himself in other important matters. He improved the marriage laws. He told parents not to arrange marriages for their children unless the young couple had met each other and thought they could be happy together. He made stern rules to obtain justice in the courts.

Rav composed a prayer to be said on New Year's Day. It is such a fine prayer that it became part of the daily service. This prayer is called "Oleinu." In beautiful language, Oleinu expresses the idea that there is one God over all the earth. The adoration service in the *Union Prayerbook* is based on Oleinu. When you say, "We pray that the day may come . . . when all who dwell on earth shall know that to Thee alone every knee must bend and every tongue give homage," you are echoing words which have been repeated in prayer since the third century.

While Rav was carrying on such a successful school at Sura, his friend, Samuel, was also doing fine work in the city of Nehardea.

Samuel was born in Nehardea but went to Palestine to study. He, too, returned to Babylonia filled with zeal and ambition. He became the head of a school in Nehardea and had many students and followers.

Samuel was a different sort of person from Rav. Rav's knowledge and study were all directed along Jewish lines. Samuel had learned the science of medicine and of astronomy, in addition to being a great Jewish scholar. He once said that he knew the paths of the sky as well as the streets of Nehardea. He used his knowledge of astronomy to work out a calendar which could serve for sixty years. He did not have to wait for messengers from Palestine to learn the dates of the festivals and of the new months. However, the patriarch was still eager to keep the authority over the calendar, and Samuel did not press him to take his calendar.

More than a hundred years later, when Hillel the Patriarch

prepared his rules for the calendar to be sent all over, he made good use of the calendar which Samuel had sent to Palestine so long before.

While Samuel was a student of Judah ha-Nasi, he prepared a salve for his teacher's eyes. This salve was helpful to Judah. In Babylonia, Samuel was often called on to help people who had trouble with their eyes.

Samuel had a sharp, clear mind. He saw that large numbers of Jews were living outside of Palestine. He felt they must become a part of the country in which they lived. He made an important statement. He declared, "The law of the land must be followed by Jews who live in that land." Samuel said this at about the year 225. Since that time, this statement has been followed by Jews in whatever land they lived.

Let us find an example. When a Jewish young couple wish to be married, they go to a rabbi. The rabbi will marry them according to the laws of their religion. However, they must first have a marriage license. The marriage license is issued by the state. That is the law of the land. The rabbi will not marry them until they have followed the law of the land.

Almost eight hundred years earlier, the prophet Jeremiah wrote to the first exiles in Babylonia, "Seek the peace of the city to which you have been carried away."

When we are law-abiding citizens of our state, we are following out Samuel's law. When we do our share for the betterment of our country, we are doing what Jeremiah thought should be done. The advice of these two leaders helped Jews to live as good citizens and faithful Jews in many lands and for many centuries.

During the lifetime of Rav and Samuel, serious events happened in Babylonia. The ruling house was overthrown. A new family of Persian rulers came to the throne. These rulers believed in the ancient religion of the Persians. Its founder was named Zoroaster. The religion is called by a long name, Zoroastrianism. In this religion, light and fire were worshipped. Its priests were also magicians. At first, the new rulers and priests made laws which were hard for others to follow. After a few years, however, these rules became less severe. Jews were able to live under the new kings as before.

A host of scholars arose in Babylonia after Rav and Samuel. As they studied the Mishnah and tried to follow its laws, they found many difficulties. Life in Babylonia was different than life in Palestine. Some laws had no meaning in the new country.

They followed in the footsteps of the teachers of long ago. Hillel had tried to find the real meaning of a Biblical law and make it work for Jews of his time. The Babylonian rabbis took the laws of the Mishnah and changed them so that they could be used in Babylonia.

These teachers were called the Amoraim. Their work influenced the life of Jews for a thousand years to come.

SOMETHING TO TALK OVER IN CLASS

What were the differences between life in Palestine and life in Babylonia?

How were the exilarchs in Babylonia and the patriarchs in Palestine similar? How were they different?

Suppose someone said, "From bitter came forth sweet." Does this make you think of the Babylonian settlement? Why?

A MAP OF ACTIVITY

On your outline map, put in the cities of Nehardea and Sura. Draw a tiny schoolhouse next to a city where a school was established.

READ

Great Men in Israel by Weis, "School Days in Babylon," p. 43; "Huna, the Generous Farmer," p. 46.

READINGS FOR TEACHERS

Unit 6 (*CHAPTERS 16–17*)

The History of the Jewish People by Margolis and Marx, Chaps. XXXVI, XXXVII.

History of the Jews, Book II, by Grayzel, Chaps. III, IV.

Jewish Post-Biblical History by Bildersee, Chap. V.

The Great Jewish Books by Samuel Caplan and Harold U. Ribalov, "The Talmud," p. 59; "Selections from the Talmud," p. 71.

The Bar Mitzvah Treasury edited by Eisenberg, "The Ordination," by Harry Sackler, p. 155.

The Responsa Literature by Solomon B. Freehof, Introduction and Chap. I, pp. 21–34.

17. THE TALMUD

THE NEW Babylonian rulers went to war, and the Jews were caught in the fighting. The Romans and the Persians were struggling bitterly. From the north beyond Syria came a fighting robber-captain. His army fell on the city of Nehardea, and destroyed it completely. The inhabitants fled to neighboring cities. After a number of years, the school was transferred to another city.

In the meantime, another great academy of learning opened in a city called Pumbeditha. The schools of Sura and Pumbeditha continued to teach for almost eight hundred years. That is a long time for a school to be open. There are not many universities in the world today which are eight hundred years old. The famous university of Oxford in England, of which you have surely heard, was begun in 1249. It is about seven hundred years old now. Harvard University in Boston recently passed its three hundredth birthday. Columbia University in New York City was two hundred years old in 1955.

Many great teachers and rabbis continued the work of the schools. The Jews were eager to send their sons to the academies. When the heads of the schools were men of wealth, they often supported a number of poor students. Those men who did not devote all their time to study went to Sura for the Kallah months. They discussed the Mishnah and the writings which had followed it. When a question of law came up, they consulted the Mishnah. It was no longer necessary to write a letter to the Sanhedrin or to the patriarch in Palestine. The law was written down in the Mishnah.

However, one important problem had to be faced. How could the laws of the Mishnah be suited to life in Babylonia? Additions and explanations to the Mishnah had to be made all the time. Long discussions took place between the rabbis and their students. A new Oral Law developed.

This new Oral Law consisted of the discussions of the rabbis, their interpretations of the Mishnah, and additions to it. These additions were called the Gemara. The Gemara was not written down. Instead of memorizing the Mishnah, as in the days before Judah ha-Nasi, the students memorized the Gemara. As a matter of fact, they usually learned the Mishnah by heart without trying because they repeated it so many times.

One of the great teachers at the academy at Sura was named Rabbi Ashi, usually called Rav Ashi. He lived from 357 to 427. During his lifetime the school at Sura rose to new heights of scholarship and importance.

When Rabbi Ashi became head of the school of Sura, he was a very young man. He had great wealth. The school was in a bad condition. Even the buildings were shabby and broken-down. Under Ashi's leadership the school grew. He put up new buildings, high on a hill. They could be seen far and wide. Once more students came to Sura. Once more the exilarch came to Sura.

Ashi saw that the Gemara had to be put in order. When the Kallah months came around, Ashi and his pupils took up the Mishnah, section by section. They searched their minds for the discussions and additions which had taken place about each section. They put them in order, according to the arrangement of the books of the Mishnah. When all the additions and explanations had been gathered and put in order, they learned them in their new arrangement. Each Mishnah, that is each question of law, was studied together with the Gemara which belonged to it and which explained it.

Fortunately Ashi had many years to do his work. He was the head of the school for fifty years. They were years of peace. There was time and opportunity for study. He made order out of the great mass of information which became the Gemara.

Then a serious threat to the lives and safety of Babylonian Jewry appeared. The Zoroastrian priests won a position of influence in the government. They persuaded the king to issue new laws against all other religions. Judaism was one of their targets. Jews were forbidden to keep the Sabbath and the festivals. The meetings of the Kallah could not be held. Some of the important rabbis were executed. Even one of the exilarchs was put to death.

Ravina, the teacher who followed Rav Ashi, came to a decision. He would wait no longer. He would take the work which Ashi had begun and he would finish it. The wisdom of the Babylonian scholars from the time of Rav and Samuel would not be forgotten. It would be written down in a complete form. It could be used by Jews wherever they lived.

Thus the great work known as the Talmud came into being. The Talmud consists of two parts—the Mishnah and the Gemara. An easy way to describe them is to say that the Mishnah is the Oral Law which explains the Bible, and the Gemara is the Oral Law which explains the Mishnah. Together they make the Talmud. Most of the Gemara is writ-

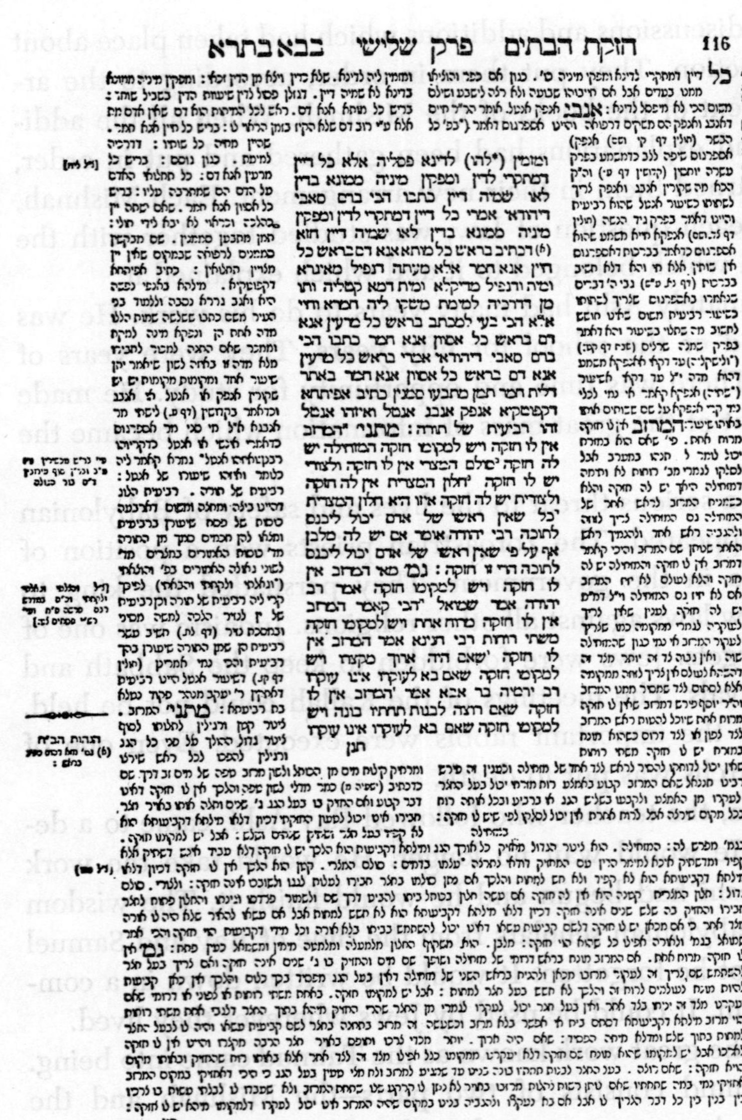
116 הזקת הבתים פרק שלישי בבא בתרא

A Page of the Talmud

ten in Aramaic with some Hebrew. You remember that the Mishnah was written in fine Hebrew.

But the Talmud is not only a book of law. It contains two kinds of writing—"Halacha," the law, and "Agaddah," story and literature. For the rabbis knew so much of Jewish history, legend, and folklore that they told many tales about the heroes of the Bible and later times. Many rabbis were learned in medicine, astronomy, and in mathematics. They used their knowledge of these sciences to help them come to a decision. Sometimes they added a wise saying or a proverb. All these lovely legends, clever sayings, and tales from the storehouse of wisdom went into the Talmud. They are the Agaddah. Often the stories of the Agaddah would make a point clear or bring out the meaning of a law.

Halacha and Agaddah might be compared to the Tigris and the Euphrates. They were the twin rivers of Jewish thought. They watered and nourished Jewish life. The Halacha answered questions of law. The Agaddah taught faith in God. Both taught righteousness between man and man.

Would you like to have an idea of what a Talmudic discussion is like? We will open a book of the Talmud. It is called "Baba Metsia." We will follow an example of Halacha.

If a man named Reuben gives Simeon an object to take care of, and then Simeon turns it over to Levi, a question arises: is Simeon still responsible for the object? Rav says he is not. Rabbi Jochanan says he is.

Rav explains: it is clear that he is not responsible if he is not being paid for watching the article and gives it to someone who is being paid, for a paid guardian is more reliable. Rav also says, the important point is not whether the second person is paid or unpaid, but whether he understands his responsibility.

Rabbi Jochanan says that is *not* the important point. Simeon is responsible no matter to whom he gives it. Why? Because Reuben can say, "It was not my desire that my object should be in the hands of anyone else. I entrusted it to Simeon."

What is the law? Should the question be decided according to Rav or according to Rabbi Jochanan?

The rabbis searched in the Mishnah. They found an earlier example of a man who promised to take care of an article and gave it over to another person. The judges at that time decided that the first man was still responsible for it. So the law of the Mishnah is according to Rabbi Jochanan's decision. In the future, if any rabbi had a case like this, he would know how to decide it.

Now we turn to a portion of the Talmud which combines Halacha and Agaddah. We will open a book called "Sanhedrin," which describes the duties and powers of the great Sanhedrin and of the small Sanhedrins. The privileges of the High Priest and of the king in the courts are related. Varying punishments for different crimes are stated. Questions dealing with judges and witnesses are considered in this volume.

"Sanhedrin" opens with a quotation from the Mishnah: Cases dealing with money must be judged by three judges; claims for full or half damages also by three. But a case of libel (speaking evil of another) requires a court of twenty-three. . . . Cases which may have the death penalty must have three judges. . . . A false prophet and a High Priest can be judged only by a court of seventy-one.

So far it is all Halacha. The law is clearly stated. Now we come to the Gemara. Remember, the Gemara is the Oral Law which developed from the Mishnah.

The Gemara examined very carefully the cases which were

to come before three judges. The laws to govern different situations were discussed. This too is Halacha.

Then comes Agaddah. The rabbis asked the question, "What is justice?" They said that sometimes strict justice may work a hardship on a person. What should be done in such a case? They chose an example from the Bible. The Bible says that "King David was just and charitable toward all his people." One rabbi explained this sentence. It may have happened, he said, that King David ordered a guilty man to pay damages to another man. But the guilty man was poor and could not pay. King David gave him the money to satisfy the judgment. In this way, he was just to the man who deserved the money, and charitable to the poor man. So justice and mercy (or charity) must go together.

The rabbis continued. They asked how should a judge act in a case between a rich man and a poor man. This time they quoted from the Book of Deuteronomy which says, "Ye shall not be afraid of the face of any man."

A story comes into this part of the discussion. It is about Rav. A man once came to Rav. Rav asked him, "What do you wish?"

"I have a case to be tried," replied the man.

"Was I not once a guest in your house?" asked Rav.

"Yes," he answered.

"If that is so," said Rav, "I cannot be the judge in your case." He turned to another rabbi and said, "Go you, and judge the case."

Another question which was discussed in this book of the Talmud was the law about how many rabbis were needed to ordain a student as a rabbi. The answer was three, but in some cases one rabbi was permitted to do so. An Agaddah about a brave rabbi who ordained five pupils came in here. The incident occurred at the time of Emperor Hadrian when he said that no teacher was permitted to ordain his pupils. If he did so his city would be destroyed and its boundaries uprooted. Rabbi Judah ben Baba took his pupils to a place hidden between two mountains and between two cities. He laid his hands on his pupils' heads and pronounced them rabbis. The Romans discovered them. Rabbi Judah ordered his pupils to flee to safety, while he remained behind and was killed by the Romans.

The Babylonian rabbis held these discussions long after the Sanhedrin had disappeared. What purpose did they have? They taught that the ideas which guided the judges of the Sanhedrin could guide judges later and in different places. And for long years to come, even after the days of Babylonia, judges went back to the pages of the Talmud, to the chapters of Sanhedrin and elsewhere, for help in judging wisely and well.

These examples from the Talmud take up about forty

pages. How would you like to have to learn so many pages by heart? Rabbi Ashi's pupils could probably recite from memory twice or three times as many pages.

The Talmud is one of the largest collections of human wisdom that has ever been prepared. It is an encyclopedia of religion and science. It is a storehouse of legend and history. It contains the thoughts of the Amoraim, the most learned rabbis of the period. The Talmud had one central thought. It was to make it possible for Jews to live honestly and justly as they had been taught by their teachers. The lessons of the Bible had to be put into every-day laws which a man could follow. The Talmud showed the way to an honorable life, based on religious ideals.

The teachers and scholars in Palestine had also prepared a Talmud. This grew up in the same way as the Babylonian Talmud. It too followed the arrangement of the Mishnah. Although it was prepared in Tiberias it is called the Jerusalem Talmud. The Jerusalem Talmud was written down at about the time of the last patriarch. The Amoraim in Palestine also decided not to depend on the memory of their pupils. The precious wisdom of the rabbis had to be kept in permanent form.

The years that came now were difficult years not only for Jews but for the great empires of the world. The Roman Empire was split. Newcomers from the north of Europe became powerful. The Parthian Empire of which Babylonia was a part was involved in wars.

A group of Babylonian Jews decided to try a new home. They traveled a long way to the land of India. The ruler welcomed them warmly. There they settled. From this group came the Indian Jews who are found in that far-off land.

At about the same time, the son of the exilarch who had

been executed by the Persians fled to Palestine. When he grew up, he became the head of the school in Tiberias and attracted students to come there.

The completion of the Talmud at about 500 marked the close of an eventful era. The schools continued to exist, but they were smaller and less important. For a while, they were not the brilliant centers of learning which they had been. For about a hundred years, no great teachers or rulers arose in Babylonia.

Then came a challenge and a threat from a new religion.

SOMETHING TO DO

From the examples of the Talmud in this chapter select the parts which are Halacha and those which are Agaddah.

Write a short composition describing the Talmud.

Examine a page of the Talmud on page 138.

TALK OVER IN CLASS

What were some reasons that made Ravina decide to write down the Talmud?

READ

World-Over Story Book, edited by Belth, "The Lost Jews of India" by Morris Epstein, p. 432.

Unit 6

Firm as a Rock

Sometimes it is good to be put to the test. If a man fights for what he believes, we are proud of him. A people and a religion can show their worth in the same way.

Two challenges faced Judaism and the Jewish people during the next five hundred years. One came from without. It was a new religion—another branch on the tree of Judaism—which took hold of a great part of the world. It threatened with the sword in order to win Jews away from their own faith.

The second challenge came from within. A group of Jews questioned the authority of the Talmud. Could Jewish life continue without the Talmud and its teachings?

These questions troubled the Jewish world for two centuries.

For Allah and Mohammed

18. FOR ALLAH AND MOHAMMED

FROM THE yellow sands of the Arabian desert, stretching over a vast area, came a new religion and a new empire. The lives of millions of people and a half-dozen countries were changed. Once again, a new faith, stemming directly from the teachings of Judaism, was born.

At the southern end of the Arabian Peninsula lies the district of Yemen. A traveler to this area between the second and the fifth centuries would find people living in tents, speaking Arabic, and wearing the long-flowing garments of the Arabs. They were grouped in tribes with a sheik as their chieftain. The sheik was ruler and judge. Among these tribes were Jews who could hardly be told from their Arab neighbors.

Jews came to Arabia after the destruction of the Temple. They lived peacefully among the Arabs. Most of them raised cattle and had small farms. On swift Arab horses they traveled over the land, free men in a vast country. Arabs and Jews were open-handed and hospitable and welcomed the stranger who came to them. The Arabs were fond of song and poetry, and the Jews of Arabia also were known for their fine poetry.

The Jews of Yemen made the long trek north over the

desert in large caravans to trade and to bargain. They came to the cities of Mecca and Yatrib. There they met other Jews. Yatrib, especially, had a large Jewish population. One tribe had a market named after it. They were goldsmiths, weavers, and traders. The visitors prayed together and learned what was happening in Jewish affairs in other lands.

The Jews of Arabia were different from their Arab neighbors in one important way. The Arabs worshipped idols. They had three hundred and sixty-five gods—one for every day of the year. The Jews worshipped one God. The Jews kept the customs and laws of their own religion. They followed the religious rulings of the patriarch. They welcomed his messengers and waited for them to bring the dates of the calendar to their settlement. They kept in touch with Babylonia and with the heads of the academies there.

Many Arabs, like the pagans of the Roman Empire, were not satisfied to be idol worshippers. They heard the early Bible stories from their Jewish friends. They believed that they were descended from Ishmael, son of Abraham. The Jews were their brethren. The teachings of Judaism seemed good to these Arabs. They were ready to cast away the worship of many gods in the form of idols. One entire tribe became Jews. They accepted the idea of one God and other Jewish teachings.

Change was in the air. A man was needed to bring people and ideas together. Mohammed, an Arab camel driver of Mecca, became the leader who brought his people a new faith and undreamed of power.

On many trips around his own land and also to Palestine, Mohammed learned about Judaism. He knew of Christianity, the other religion, which had come from the Jewish faith. Mohammed believed in the main teachings of Judaism. He followed many Jewish customs and laws. First and foremost was the belief in one God, called Allah. Abraham, Isaac, and Jacob were the patriarchs of the new religion, too. Mohammed accepted Moses as a prophet, and believed that Jesus was a prophet, too. He declared that he, Mohammed, was the greatest prophet of all. His watchword was, "There is no God but Allah, and Mohammed is His prophet." This was the corner-stone of his new religion. It was called Islam or Mohammedanism. Its followers were Moslems or Mohammedans.

Mohammed knew the Jews who lived in Mecca. He may have traveled with others as they crossed the desert in caravans. Perhaps over a camp fire, at an oasis, he heard the tales of the Bible. He may have made his plans looking at the starry sky in the quiet of the desert night.

Back in Mecca, Mohammed gathered people around him and spoke to them of his new religious ideas. He asked them to stop worshipping idols and to follow the ideas of better living which he taught. Some people were impressed. Others laughed or were angry.

At first Mohammed made little headway. He was forced to leave Mecca. He fled to Yatrib, the home of the large Jewish settlement. This happened in the year 622, which became a very important date for Moslems. Their calendar begins with this date. For them, it is the year 1. The city of Yatrib received a new name. From that time on, it has been called Medina, "The City of the Prophet."

Mohammed expected the large Jewish population of Medina and the Jews in the rest of Arabia to rally to his side. He was mistaken. The Jews had no reason to change their religion, or to accept Mohammed as a prophet. They saw that Islam was an improvement over paganism. But what could it give them that they did not already have in Judaism? Their faith was dear to them, and they were ready to defend it.

Mohammed became a bitter enemy of the Jews. With armed followers, he fell on the Jewish tribes, one by one, and overpowered them. Some of them had to leave Arabia. Others remained, but never again as free citizens. He changed some of the customs of his religion which he had copied from the Jews. For example, Moslems had been told to turn toward Jerusalem when they prayed. Now he instructed them to turn toward Mecca. Mohammed had put the Day of Atonement, Yom Kippur, into the Moslem calendar. He took it out and made new rules for fasting.

With swords in hands, and the cry of "Allah and Mohammed" on their lips, the Moslems poured over Arabia. To die in the cause of Islam was a holy death, and they were reckless in battle. They swept before them the people of their own land and moved on to other countries. They conquered Syria, Palestine, Persia, and Egypt. The sword made converts of people and rulers. A vast Arabian Empire was created based on the new religion. In time it reached westward to

Spain and almost as far east as China. Before Mohammed died in 632 he saw the beginning of Moslem rule over a great part of the world.

Once again the seeds of Judaism had brought the belief in one God and the teachings of the Bible to millions of people.

SOME QUESTIONS TO ANSWER

How did Islam come into being?
What did Mohammed call himself?
What do Moslems call God?
What did both Islam and Christianity take from Judaism?
How did Islam make a tremendous number of converts?
Why did Mohammed become angry with the Jews?

A MAP ACTIVITY

Find Arabia on the map on page 162. On your own map, outline Arabia. Put in the cities of Bagdad, Mecca, and Medina. You may call Medina by its other name if you wish.

READ

The Great March, Book I, by Lurie, "As Faithful as That," p. 109.

READINGS FOR TEACHERS

Unit 6 (*CHAPTERS 18–20*)

A History of the Jewish People by Margolis and Marx, Chaps. XXXVII–XLI.

History of the Jews, Book II, by Grayzel, Chaps. V–VIII.

Jewish Post-Biblical History by Bildersee, Chaps. V, VI.

A Treasury of Jewish Letters, Vol. I, edited by Franz Kobler, "Letters of Saadia Gaon," p. 78.

The Jew in the Medieval World by Marcus, #47 "Anan and the Rise of Karaism," p. 233; #57 "Saadia," p. 287.

19. UNDER THE MOSLEMS

THE CAPITAL of the new empire was the city of Bagdad. The king was called the Caliph. Stories you may have read, like those in the "Arabian Nights," tell of the wealth and luxury in which the caliph and his courtiers lived.

A time of prosperity began for those ruled by the caliphs. Caravans hauled rich cargoes of gold and precious stones, perfume and spices, silks and woven goods from country to country. Merchants did a thriving trade in goods and supplies. Rich people built new homes. Members of the royal family erected palaces. Artisans had plenty of work. Shopkeepers and farmers sold their wares in markets and bazaars.

Over a million Jews came under Moslem rule. Their fortunes improved because they were part of a great empire which stretched over land and sea. Only their differing religions brought difficulties. In Arabia the Jews had refused to become Moslems. Jews in other lands stood just as firm.

The Moslem rulers passed a number of new laws. No new synagogues could be built. No repairs could be made to old ones. No Jew was permitted to ride a horse. He was allowed to ride only a mule or a donkey. Jews paid special taxes and extra rents for their lands. They were forbidden to wear rings. They were told to sing in subdued tones, and to pray silently for their dead. Christians had to observe these laws, too.

The new laws made some changes in Jewish life in Babylonia. Because of an extra rent tax on land, many Jews gave up farming. Only a few Jewish families of wealthy landowners remained. Jews became merchants and traders. Others were financial agents to Arab merchants and to the caliphs. They used a new device called a bill of exchange to send money from land to land. Nowadays we would call them bankers. A number of Jews became rich and important, although as usual the majority of the people were workers, small tradesmen, and farmers.

Babylonian Jews found life better under the new rulers than under the last Persian kings who had oppressed them. When the caliphs found that the Jews could perform valuable services they did not always enforce their own laws. The caliph restored the exilarch to his position of authority. He represented the Jews at court, collected taxes, and appointed judges. The caliph granted the exilarch many favors. He was permitted to wear a signet ring. He probably used the ring to seal his decrees, as was the custom in those days.

The schools of Sura and Pumbeditha reopened. The exilarchs shared their authority and dignity with the heads of the academies. The head of a school now had the title of "Gaon," or "Excellency," instead of "Rabbi." The plural of the word "Gaon" is "Geonim."

An imposing ceremony took place in the synagogue when the exilarch was installed in his office. The geonim of both Sura and Pumbeditha came to do honor to the new official. The most important men of the city went with the exilarch to the synagogue. Great crowds of people filled the building and joined in the service. Special prayers of thanksgiving were said. A new prince had come to rule over the Children of Israel!

The position of gaon also became very important. Although the gaon of Sura had the highest position of all, the gaon of Pumbeditha was also given great respect. The geonim of Babylonia became the religious leaders of the Jews. From other lands Jews came to them with their questions and their problems. Jews who had settled in new countries had to deal with different people and with untried conditions. They needed help and guidance in order to keep the ceremonies and laws of Judaism which were dear to them. They turned to the geonim for assistance.

Messengers came from far-off lands with letters from the rabbi or from the head of a community. They asked, "May we do this?" or "How shall we answer this question?" They might have inquired, "May we stop this custom? What is the law?" With the question, the messenger would bring a gift for the gaon or his school.

The letters answering these questions had a special name. They were called "Responsa." During the Kallah months the geonim and their scholars and assistants went over the questions which came from far and near. Their task was to solve the problems in accordance with Talmudic law. When they came to a decision, they wrote a letter of explanation, and gave it to the messenger to take back home. Thousands of knotty problems were solved.

The answers to these questions were usually found in the Talmud or in the writings which followed the Talmud. You may ask, why did not the rabbi search through the Talmud himself for the answer? There is a simple reason why he could not do this. There were probably only a few copies of the complete Talmud in the world. In the years before printing was invented, it may have taken years to copy a Talmud by hand. Such a copy was probably found only in the large schools. In addition—and this was even more important—the gaon had authority. His answer was based on great knowledge, gained through years of study. Jews all over were ready to follow his advice and his rulings.

The Responsa teach us a great deal. Many of them were saved and have been gathered into books. The questions which were asked and the answers which were given tell a great deal of the history of the times. They describe what occupations Jews followed. They tell which settlements lived in peace and which were disturbed. Names of places are sometimes mentioned. Reports on schools and how they taught the Torah are given. The questions and answers of the Responsa lift the veil from places and people. Without the Responsa we might never have known about them.

In later years, rabbis continued to answer questions of law by letter. From land to land, scholars received and answered questions. Men who never saw each other became friends. Jews of different cities followed the rulings of famous rabbis.

The power of the geonim was an influence for good. Their names became known far and wide. Scattered Jews felt a sense of unity. They knew that in one place there were great religious leaders to whom they could turn. The gaon became a symbol of "K'lal Yisroel," a united Jewish people.

Though many changes came to Babylonian Jews during

Moslem rule, they were not as striking as those which could be seen in Palestine. There the Jews found the Moslems kinder than their Christian rulers had been. Jews were permitted to return to Jerusalem and to live there. New groups came to Palestine, many of them from Arabia. The schools, especially in Tiberias, flourished once more. Where once the Psalmist sang, inspiration came again. Religious poems were written and added to the synagogue service. Some were sung or chanted. These songs and poems were used not only in Palestine. They became part of the worship in many lands. A number of the Rosh Ha-shono and Yom Kippur poems written at this time are read in the synagogues of our own time on these important days.

The study of the Bible came to the fore again. For many years it had been second in importance to the Talmud. The Moslems were very much interested in the Bible. They had questions to ask. Parts of it became sacred to them, just as the Bible is sacred to Christians. Now the Jews of Palestine returned to it and rediscovered its beauty and wisdom. They worked out a way to protect the Bible from changes, so that the wonderful words of our teachers would not be altered.

The scholars in Tiberias helped to make it possible for you, today, to learn to read Hebrew easily. Up to this time, Hebrew had been written only with consonants. In Tiberias, they began the system of adding to the consonants the little marks which stand for vowels. To help you understand what

שמע ישראל

שְׁמַע יִשְׂרָאֵל

they did, let us take an example in English. We begin with two consonants, "p-l." If we insert five vowel sounds between them, we can make five different words. They are, pale, peel, pile, pole, and pull. Without the vowels, there is a problem. What is the correct word? You would have to figure it out from the meaning of the entire sentence. The problem is just the same in Hebrew. The vowel signs make Hebrew reading easier for all of us.

The simple addition of vowel signs also helped to start a new branch of learning—Hebrew grammar. Rules of Hebrew grammar had not been written before. Now scholars turned their attention to this important field to help students write correct Hebrew. Much fine writing came from Palestine during this period.

For a hundred years Jews lived quietly under the Moslems. Talmudic scholarship flourished in Babylonia under the geonim. Poetry and a new interest in the Bible came from Palestine. Then came a change. Undercurrents which had been gathering strength for some time rose to the surface. The Jewish world was faced with a crisis.

TALK OVER IN CLASS

How did the Jews of Babylonia fare under Moslem rulers?

How did the Jews of Palestine fare under Moslem rulers?

Compare the position of gaon with the position of exilarch. Which do you think was more important? Why?

READ

The Bar Mitzvah Treasury edited by Eisenberg, "The Tallit Weaver of Bagdad" by David Frishman, p. 112.

Watchmen of the Night by Kalisher, "In a Persian Garden," p. 28.

The Heaven on the Sea by Sulamith Ish-Kishor, "The Sabbath Pearls," p. 101.

20. A GREAT LEADER

DO YOU remember the Sadducees? They believed that Jews should live by the laws of the Bible alone, without changes, additions, or explanations.

A group of Jews in Babylonia arose who remind us of the Sadducees. They, too, looked to the Bible for laws to live by. Their name, the Karaites, means "Followers of the Bible."

The Karaites set aside the rulings of the Mishnah and the Gemara. They would not follow the geonim and the rabbis and scholars who taught according to the Talmud.

Such a movement does not grow up over night. For many years there had been dissatisfaction with the exilarch and the geonim. The taxes which the exilarch collected bore down heavily on poor people. Some Jews dreamed of seeing Palestine restored to its former glory. They hoped it would be governed as it once had been by the laws of the Bible. Hopes, dreams, and discontent came together, when a leader was found. His name was Anan ben David.

Anan was an educated man. One story about him says that he was a brother of the exilarch. The movement he led was organized at about the year 765.

Because the Karaites believed only in Biblical law, their life was different from the lives of those who continued to follow the Torah according to the Talmud. Their observance of the Sabbath day is a good example of Karaite ways of life.

On the Sabbath they did not permit any lights in their homes. They obeyed the words of the Bible which said: "Ye shall kindle no fire throughout your habitations upon the Sabbath Day." Those who followed the Talmud would permit a non-Jew to light the lamp and the fire for them, or they lit them before the Sabbath began. The homes of the Karaites were dark and cold on the Sabbath eve. They ate no hot foods during the Sabbath, and left their homes only for the synagogue. They did not visit family or friends on the Sabbath.

In general, the Karaites led a gloomy life. They felt that until Zion was restored, Jews should not be happy. Many more fast days were observed by them during the year. They went back to the Bible to fix the calendar and would not rely on the science of astronomy. They waited for the new moon to appear to declare a new month. They did not believe in doctors. They thought that faith in God was enough to cure a sick person.

Anan ben David declared, "Search thoroughly in the Bible." He did not order people to follow his opinion, but wanted them to study the Bible for themselves. He also said that every man had a right to decide for himself the meaning of the Bible. Such a ruling would surely bring difficulties to the Jews. Karaite leaders who came after Anan differed with him, and even began to follow some Talmudic laws.

For Anan and his followers forgot one important fact. The Talmud was not created at one time. It was the work of scholars who lived over a period of many years. The laws of the Bible were written for people who lived a simple life in their own country. Most of them were farmers and shepherds. Jews of later times lived in many different lands and engaged in many different kinds of work. The laws of the

Bible had to be explained even in Palestine before the Temple fell. A thousand years of history, in and out of Palestine, created the Talmud. It made Judaism a religion that could change and grow. The Karaites forgot their own history.

The Karaite movement spread to Egypt and Syria. Later on a large number of Karaites moved into eastern Europe. As late as 1925, and probably up to World War II, a small group of Karaites lived in Troki, in Lithuania.

In our own time, a hundred Karaite families are working as farmers in a village near Tel Aviv in Israel. They grow fruit trees and olive trees. Scattered groups of Karaites are found in other parts of Israel. Jerusalem still has five Karaite families who are directly descended from the group which lived in Jerusalem back in early Moslem days.

The prayer books of the Karaites and the dates of the festivals are different from ours. However, the Karaites are welcomed as descendants of our own people and as followers of the Bible.

Karaism stirred up Jewish life during the ninth and tenth centuries. It made people ask questions. It put the geonim and the rabbis on their mettle. Karaite scholars also wrote interesting and worth while books, poems and prayers. One important and valuable result of the Karaite movement was that the Bible was read and studied more than it had been for years. The Karaites wrote fine Hebrew grammars and commentaries, or explanations of the Bible. But Karaism did not appeal to the Jews as a whole. Karaism looked backward. The Jewish people looked forward. They could not only mourn for the past. They had to look ahead and try to live a vigorous Jewish life wherever they were.

While Karaism was still causing discussion and even strife in Jewish life, Babylonian Jewry faced a new test. A final attempt was made in Palestine to take over the position of Jewish leadership. How could this be done? By scholarship? No. The geonim still were called on to send out responsa to Jews in communities all over the world. By wealth? No. The Jews of Palestine could not compete with Babylonian Jews in riches.

Have you guessed how? It was through the calendar. The calendar had always brought unity to the Jewish world. To fix the calendar was the sign of Jewish leadership. Suddenly, Aaron ben Meir, a scholar of Tiberias, where schools were stronger than ever before, questioned the correctness of the Babylonian calendar. He sent out a calendar of his own. According to the Palestinian calendar of that year, Passover fell on Sunday. According to the Babylonian calendar, Passover fell on Tuesday. For three years, Jews in different lands celebrated holidays on different days.

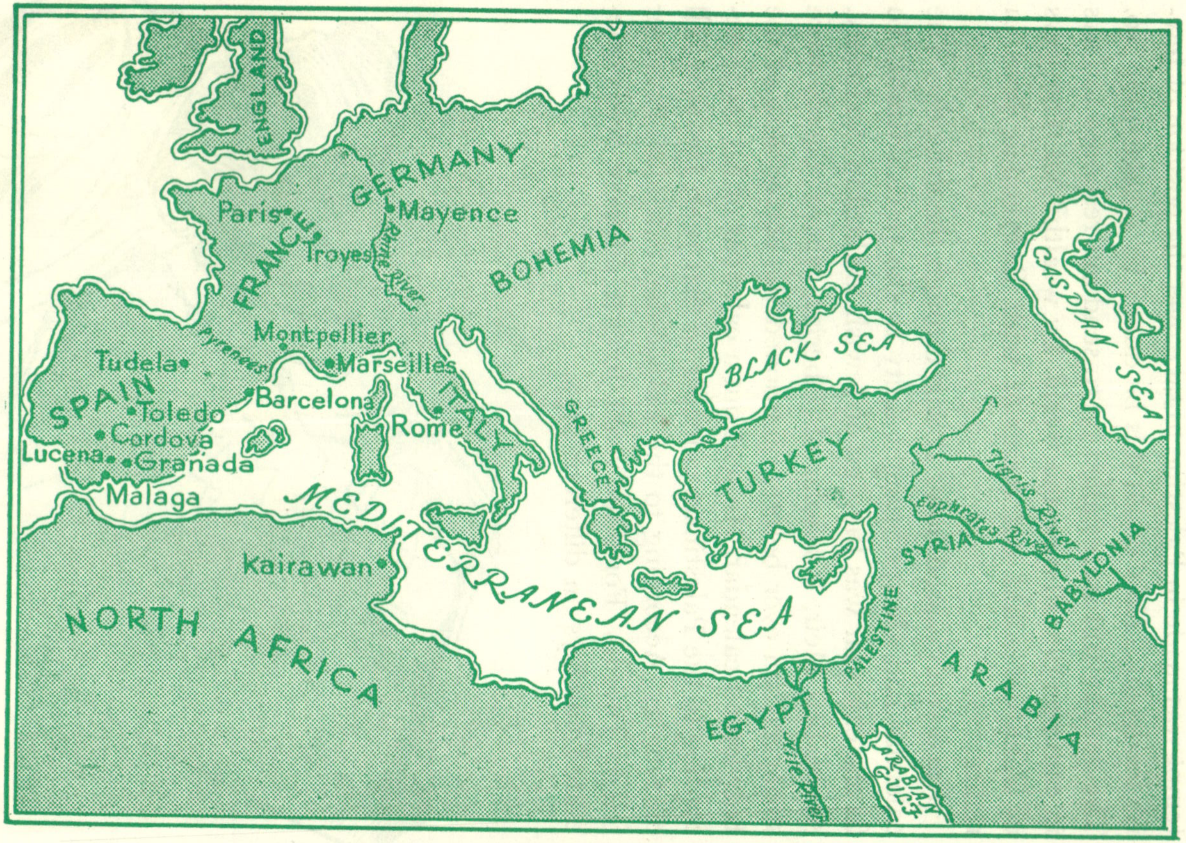

Centers of Jewry in the Middle Ages

The school at Sura was without a head. A leader had to be found who could deal with the question of the Karaites and clear up the confusion about the calendar.

The man who became the leader of Babylonian Jewry was not a member of the important or scholarly families. He came neither from Babylonia nor from Palestine. He was born in Egypt in 892. His name was Saadiah ben Joseph.

When Saadiah was still a very young man, he wrote a fine Hebrew grammar which was helpful to students of the Bible. From then on, he wrote numerous articles, letters, and books. Many of them were about the Karaites, who were growing very strong. He examined their ideas which he felt were harmful to the future of Judaism. A great many people lost their interest in Karaism after reading Saadiah's articles. From Saadiah's time on, Karaism gained fewer followers and became less important.

Saadiah was dismayed to learn that Ben Meir had sent out a calendar of his own. He feared that Jews would be confused. They might work on holidays. They might eat forbidden food during the days of Passover. He wrote letters to his pupils telling them to be on guard. Wherever he went he

spoke against the Palestinian calendar. He wrote to the exilarch offering to help.

The exilarch asked Saadiah to prepare a book about the holidays and festivals. Saadiah wrote a volume called, *The Book of the Seasons.* After this book appeared, the question of the calendar was settled forever. One calendar, fixed according to Jewish laws and based on the science of astronomy, served all Jews.

Saadiah displayed so much knowledge by his letters and writings that he was asked to come to Babylonia to become the gaon of Sura. He became known as Saadiah Gaon, as though the title was part of his name. He was the greatest religious teacher of his time.

Among the many letters which Saadiah Gaon wrote, one went to a settlement of Jews in Egypt. Although he addressed the letter to one settlement, he must have felt that he was speaking to Jews all over. In this letter he advised them to be righteous, to be faithful to the teachings of the Torah, and to pray to God. He reminded them to study, and offered to help them in time of need. His letter is filled with quotations from the Bible and the Talmud. It shows Saadiah's great knowledge, his love for his people, and his desire to lead them well.

Only two years after Saadiah became gaon he was put to a serious test. The exilarch had judged a case and had come to a decision. The geonim were supposed to sign the judgments of the exilarchs. Saadiah did not believe the decision was fair or just. He refused to sign the papers.

The exilarch was angry. He thought Saadiah would obey him since he had appointed him gaon. For seven years Saadiah and the exilarch opposed each other. During this time, Saadiah had to leave Sura to live in Bagdad.

However, Saadiah Gaon was a very busy man. He lived at a time when Bagdad, the capital of the Moslem world, was the center of education and culture. The caliphs were liberal rulers. They wanted their people to learn from the nations which they conquered.

Saadiah combined general knowledge with Jewish education. He wrote and taught in many fields. He worked unceasingly. He was the first to translate the Bible into Arabic. With the translation, he prepared explanations of many of the books of the Bible. Thousands of people who knew only Arabic were now able to read and study the Bible. Among them were Arabs as well as Jews. For the second time, the Bible entered a world of brilliant thought. The Septuagint brought the Bible to the Greek-speaking people. Saadiah's translation opened it to a host of new Arabic readers.

Saadiah's position was very much like the position of Philo, the Jewish thinker of Alexandria. They both had to answer questions about God and Judaism for the Jews and non-Jews of their day. Philo lived among Greeks and Saadiah lived in an Arabic world. Saadiah wrote a great book called *Beliefs and Opinions.* His purpose was to make Judaism clear to all who wished to know, and to explain how a man of education and science could have faith and trust in God.

There is hardly a field in which Saadiah Gaon did not write. He composed poems and prayers. He was an authority on Hebrew grammar. He wrote letters and responsa answering questions on the Bible and the Talmud. After his death in 942, no scholar appeared for more than two hundred years who could equal him.

The academies of Sura and Pumbeditha remained open for another hundred years. Then they closed forever. The fortunes of the Jews were intertwined with the fortunes of the rulers of the country, the caliphs of Bagdad. As their wealth and power lessened, the strength of the Jewish settlement became less. The Moslem Empire was no longer one great union. Egypt had a caliph of its own. So did North Africa.

The Jewish scholars of Babylonia began to go to other lands. They carried the Torah with them. They became the rabbis and teachers of new settlements. Wherever they went, schools and synagogues opened. In North Africa and in Central Europe, there were many Jewish settlements. In Spain a great Jewish community began to take shape. In Italy Jews held a strong position. As the world grew larger, Jews pushed out further.

Babylonia's day was over. The Babylonian center had been a pillar of strength. The teaching of its great scholars, especially the Talmud, was to be the corner-stone of Jewish life for years to come. Now Babylonia gave up its position to the young and vigorous settlements of Europe.

WRITE A COMPOSITION

The Babylonian teacher I admire most is ________________.
You may select Rav, Samuel, Rabbi Ashi, Ravina, or Saadiah.
Think of the important work which each man did to help you decide on the subject. Put yourself in his place.

WHAT DO YOU THINK?

Select two members of the class. One is to be a Karaite; one is to be a Rabbanite (follower of the Talmudic rabbis). Each one must try to win over the class to his ideas of Judaism. When they have finished, the class may ask them questions or add new points to their arguments.

READ

The Great March, Book I, by Lurie, "Even Though I Lose," p. 122.

Watchmen of the Night by Kalisher, "The First Philosopher," p. 32.

Unit 7

The Golden Age

What makes a "Golden Age"? Perhaps the "Four Freedoms" mentioned by President Franklin D. Roosevelt sum up what is necessary to bring about a Golden Age. They are freedom of speech, freedom of religion, freedom from want, and freedom from fear.

In southern Spain beginning with the tenth century and for at least two hundred years, the Jews had these four freedoms. They lived with their neighbors at ease. For the most part the Moors (the Arabs of Spain) respected the Jews and sought their friendship. Many were prosperous. Those who were not were helped by their fellow Jews. Except for short lapses of time, there was religious freedom.

The Four Freedoms alone did not make a Golden Age. To these were added the traditions of the Jewish people, the joy of learning, and the genius which flowered in poetry and in science.

Let us see if you agree that the next period deserved the name, the "Golden Age."

Maimonides, the Healer

21. BEGINNINGS IN SPAIN

WHEN YOU hear the word "Spain," what does it bring to your mind? Is it the discovery of America, a bull-fight, or a fine poem?

For Jews, Spain has two associations. One is very, very good, and one is very, very bad. The first words which come to mind are "Golden Age." The next words are "The Inquisition." Between these two phrases were five hundred years of history. They were years of glorious accomplishment. Even when they came to an end, their treasures were not lost. They became a part of our Jewish heritage.

From the early days of the Common Era when Rome held sway over the Mediterranean world, Jews lived in Spain. They had farms and vineyards. Those who lived near the coast carried on trade across the Mediterranean Sea, where thriving Jewish cities were established in North Africa. For many years, kings were gracious to their Jewish subjects and peasants were friends with their Jewish neighbors. It was the custom for a farmer to have his fields blessed before he began his planting. If a priest could not come, a pious Jew might be asked to give the blessing. Later, when the Church of Rome became powerful, the Jews suffered in the same way as the Jews of Palestine from laws which were passed against them.

All this changed, however, at the time of the Moslem conquest which spread from Arabia east and west. At first the caliph at Bagdad ruled a tremendous empire, but Spain soon broke away. By 755, an independent caliph ruled in Cordova. Cordova became the center of government, of religion, of education, and of science.

The southern part of Spain is called Andalusia. In this lovely region, some of the happiest and most fruitful years of Jewish history were spent. The cities of Cordova, Seville, Granada and further north, Toledo, had large and important settlements. To this day, these cities bear the marks of their former Jewish inhabitants, though they were driven out more than four hundred years ago. A street in Seville is called "Calle de los Levies," the Street of the Levites. In Cordova, a winding path stops at an old house which has the word "Juderia" on its side. This was the entrance to the ancient Jewish section of the city. An open square in Cordova is called "Maimonides Square," after the great Jewish philosopher whom Spain now wishes to honor. The street on which a fine synagogue stood seven hundred years ago in Toledo is called "The Street of the Synagogue," although the synagogue long

ago became a church. Spain has not forgotten its Jews and Jews cannot forget Spain.

The story of the Golden Age begins in Cordova. The city was beautiful. Lovely parks, imposing palaces, and decorated mosques were built by the Moslem conquerors. Gorgeous flowers grew easily in the mild climate. It is easy to imagine the palaces of the caliphs surrounded by large and spacious gardens with fountains and tiny lakes, cared for by faithful attendants.

Under the Moslems, a new and fresh breeze swept over Jewish life. The Arabs in Spain, like those in Bagdad, thirsted for knowledge. They were eager to learn the secrets of astronomy, of mathematics and of medicine. They paid homage to the poet and the writer. They formed a bond of kinship with the Jews whose love of learning and skill in science and poetry were so similar to theirs.

Before long Jews came to Spain in large numbers. They were merchants and traders, craftsmen and artisans, physicians and financiers. Many of them combined more than one skill. The physician was often adviser to the caliph and the scientist could write poetry, explain the Talmud, and quote the Bible.

The first of these many-sided Jewish personalities was Chasdai ibn Shaprut, who was born in Cordova at about 915. Chasdai was a man to stir the imagination. He was a physician, a writer, a financier, and a diplomat. In addition, he was a Jewish scholar and head of the community of Cordova. Officially he was physician to the caliph and inspector of the customs. Unofficially, he was the caliph's chief adviser.

Chasdai proved his value to the caliph many times. Once the emperor at Constantinople sent an embassy to Cordova with rich and beautiful gifts. Among them was a medical book written in Greek. No one at the court could read Greek. However, the book was finally translated into Latin. Then Chasdai, who was master of Arabic, Hebrew, and Latin, translated it into Arabic to the delight of the caliph.

Chasdai was sent on many a mission by his royal master. At one time he combined his duties as ambassador with his skill as a physician. He visited a small kingdom in the north and smoothed out its troubled affairs. He found that the king was sick and cured him. In return the grateful king came down to the court of the caliph. This was considered a diplomatic triumph for Chasdai.

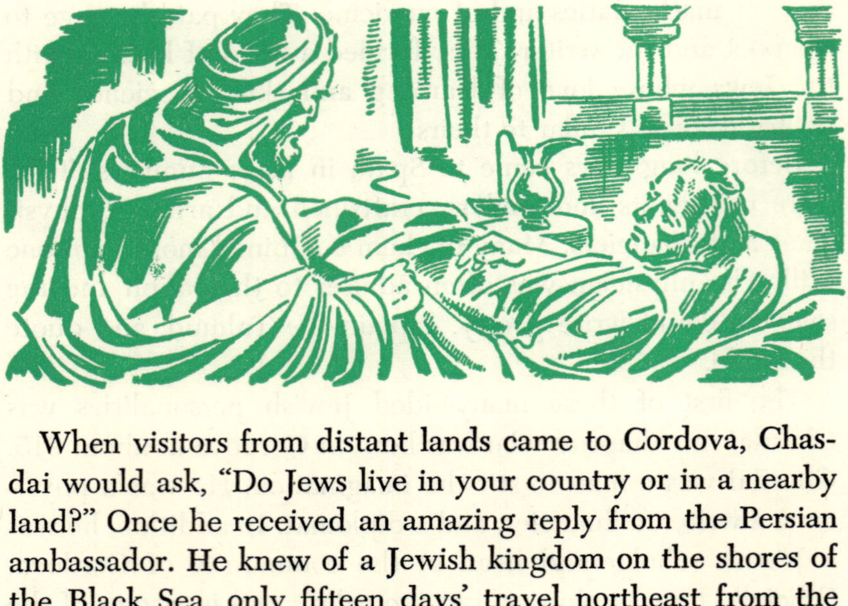

When visitors from distant lands came to Cordova, Chasdai would ask, "Do Jews live in your country or in a nearby land?" Once he received an amazing reply from the Persian ambassador. He knew of a Jewish kingdom on the shores of the Black Sea, only fifteen days' travel northeast from the city of Constantinople. The ruler was named Joseph. His people were called the Khazars. Ibn Shaprut was determined to learn more about the kingdom of the Khazars. He asked a fine Hebrew writer to help him prepare a good letter to King

Joseph, telling him about the Jews of Spain and begging him to answer. When the letter was ready, he found a messenger to take it through Constantinople to the royal city of the Khazars.

At Constantinople the messenger received bad news. He was told that his journey was too dangerous. The countries he had to pass through were at war. The seas were stormy. The letter came back to Spain. Chasdai was not discouraged. He sent the letter out once more. It went a long and roundabout way, from hand to hand, from friend to friend. Finally after more than two years had gone by, it actually arrived at the court of King Joseph.

Three more years passed until Ibn Shaprut received a reply. King Joseph was overjoyed to hear that Jews of other lands were interested in his people. He wrote a long letter telling how the king of the Khazars became dissatisfied with paganism in the year 740. After listening to a Christian, a Moslem, and a Jew, he decided to accept Judaism. The royal family, most of the nobility, and many of the people adopted Judaism.

King Joseph's interesting letter described his land and his people. He told how he awaited the return of the Jewish people to Zion and quoted from the Bible to strengthen his words. He invited Ibn Shaprut to come for a visit and promised him a royal welcome. Ibn Shaprut could not accept the invitation.

The story of the Khazars is not a legend or a tale of fancy. The letter of King Joseph is not the only evidence of their existence. Historians of other people, Arabs who wrote at the same time, mention them in their writings. Not long after the correspondence with Ibn Shaprut, the Khazars were overcome by Russian tribes. They ceased to exist as an independent nation and disappeared into the vastness of Russia.

Spanish Jewry now began to take a leading part in Jewish scholarship. Up to this time, no famous Jewish teachers were found in Spain. The story of the first great Jewish scholar in Spain is exciting. It begins back in Babylonia in the city of Sura. The school was struggling. Times were bad. Four Jewish scholars went as messengers to different places to ask for money to help the academy. Not one of the messengers returned to Sura. Their ship was captured by pirates.

After long adventures, each of them found refuge in a different city. One teacher came to Cairo, and one to Kairawan in North Africa. It is said that one of them came to southern France, and the last one arrived in Cordova. In each of the cities where the travelers settled they became teachers or heads of schools.

Moses ben Chanoch was the name of the scholar who made his way to Spain. He was held captive by a Spanish admiral who was probably a pirate. The admiral must have known that Jews were always ready to redeem a Jewish captive. Some communities had special funds set aside for this purpose. To pay for a Jewish slave and set him free was considered a mitzvah, or "good deed." An ancient law said that if there were a question about using money to redeem a slave or toward building a synagogue, the redemption of the slave came first.

Dressed in shabby clothes, worn and travel-stained, with his young son by his side, Moses ben Chanoch was put up for sale in the slave market by the admiral. The Jews of Cordova paid the admiral his price, and the traveler was freed.

Moses did not tell anyone he was a learned rabbi. As soon as he was free he went to the synagogue. He stood quietly by the door, listening. A lesson in Talmud was going on. When the rabbi had trouble answering a question, Moses asked if

he might say a word of explanation. Everyone looked up in surprise. Could this poor stranger do better than their own rabbi? Yes, he could. In only a few minutes, they realized that a fine scholar had come to their city. With great honesty, the rabbi rose and declared, "You are my teacher. You must take my place as rabbi."

The admiral soon learned that his captive was more valuable than he had supposed. He tried to get a higher ransom. The Jews appealed to the caliph. Ibn Shaprut put the case before him. The caliph was very happy to learn that a great scholar had come to Cordova. He hoped that a school would be opened in his city. He sent the admiral away empty-handed.

The caliph's hopes were realized. Moses ben Chanoch became the head of a Talmudic academy. Ibn Shaprut helped by sending to Sura for additional copies of the Talmud.

Instead of traveling all the way to Babylonia, students came to Cordova. Jewish learning was provided for side by side with Moslem culture. The years to come showed the fruits of these two avenues of knowledge.

SOMETHING TO TALK OVER IN CLASS

What would you consider a "Golden Age"?

What was more important—the letters between Chasdai ibn Shaprut and King Joseph, or the arrival of Moses ben Chanoch in Cordova? Why?

HOW TO SEND A LETTER

What various means of transportation were used to send a letter from Europe to Asia in the days of Ibn Shaprut? How would such a letter be sent today?

READ

The Great March, Book I, by Lurie, "A Gift to the Caliph," p. 126.

READINGS FOR TEACHERS

Unit 7 (*CHAPTERS 21–24*)

A History of the Jews, Book III, by Grayzel, Chap. III.

A History of the Jewish People by Margolis and Marx, Chaps. XLV, XLVI, XLVIII, XLIX.

A Treasury of Jewish Letters by Kobler, "Chasdai Ibn Shaprut's Correspondence with Joseph"; "King of the Khazars," p. 97; "Maimonides to the Jews of Yemen," p. 183; "Maimonides to Joseph Ibn Aknin," p. 203; "Maimonides to Samuel Ibn Tibbon," p. 208.

The Great Jewish Books by Caplan and Ribalov, "The Kuzari," p. 133.

22. DAY BY DAY

SOME DAY you may take a trip to Europe, to Israel, or to South America. In the cities you visit, you take a tour with a sightseeing company. Your guide will show you tall buildings, art galleries, ancient palaces, or ruined cities. That is a good day's tour.

But if you have time, you will rise early the next day to go by yourself for your own private tour of the city. You will visit the markets, you will stroll on the boulevards, you will eat at a restaurant where English is *not* spoken, and you will enter some shops and look about quietly. At the end of a day or two of such "walking tours," you will begin to know something about the city and its people. If you have read the history of the country you will understand why the people act as they do, and why they differ from folk in other lands.

Let us take a walking tour of one of the Spanish cities where Jews lived during the years between 1000 and 1300. This is an imaginary city. It combines the different elements which were found in more than one city. Cordova and Granada were in the south and Toledo was located in the center of the Spanish Peninsula. Only Jews lived in Lucena. However, certain ways of life were followed by all Jews. A general pattern of Jewish life existed for many years all over Spain. Some years were better when a ruler was kind and other years were bad when kings were at war or religious leaders spoke against the Jews.

Most Jews lived together in one section of the town. They were not forced to live there; they preferred to be near their fellow Jews. The center of their life was the synagogue, and no one wanted to be too far away.

The synagogue was usually the largest and finest building in the Jewish quarter. It was often of Moorish style, with tiny colored mosaics decorating the façade, and stately columns making archways from room to room inside. One synagogue still standing in Toledo has three rows of Hebrew phrases taken from the Bible carved into the stone, running around the four walls in a continuous frieze.

The synagogue was set in a courtyard, beautified with flowers and shaded with trees. Nearby were other buildings, used by all Jews—the schoolhouse, the assembly hall, and an inn where wayfarers might spend the night.

The synagogue was also the courthouse. Jews tried their own cases, according to Jewish law. The judges were elected or chosen by the people, and would be men learned in the law, with the rabbi acting as the court of appeal.

If we entered the synagogue of our imaginary city we would see how it was the center of Jewish life. It was not only a place of worship. Reports of the Jewish governing council were read out when all Jews were assembled. The king's decrees, good or bad, were announced there, too. Lost and found articles could be reported at some time during the service. A sale of a house or other property was not legal unless it was made known to the "Kahal" or congregation when they were all together. If a man gave a fine gift to charity, it was also announced in the synagogue.

The rabbi was the leader of the congregation. If there was more than one rabbi in the city, the oldest or the most learned was considered the chief rabbi. The rabbis carried on the tradition of unpaid leadership which went back to the days of the Sanhedrin. Many of them were physicians, and some had humbler occupations such as artisans and traders. Rabbis in most Jewish communities were not paid until the fourteenth century. It became clear then that being a rabbi was a full-time job. A rabbi who performed all his duties could not do additional work to earn a living.

Second in importance to the rabbi was the chazan, or cantor. He, too, was learned in Jewish subjects and of course had to sing well. The chazan was often a scribe. He may have copied Hebrew books and helped the rabbi in his correspondence with other cities. The chazan was paid for his work.

Now let us see how a Spanish boy—we shall call him Samuel Ibn Abraham—was educated.

Samuel began his schooling when he was three or four

years old. He was usually taught at home by a private teacher. If his family was wealthy, they lived in a fine house set in a courtyard which was entered through iron gates. A garden or orchard would surround the house. Poorer families shared a house, but even they had a courtyard and flowers to brighten it up.

From the time he was four to when he was six or seven, Samuel studied Hebrew and the Bible. Then he began the Mishnah and the Gemara. He learned to chant the Torah. If he had a sweet voice, he might have the privilege of chanting the Torah in the synagogue on Shabos. His parents would gladly make a contribution to the synagogue for the privilege.

As Samuel grew up, he probably learned Hebrew grammar, Arabic, mathematics, astronomy, or medicine. Many Jews became physicians. It was not necessary to attend a university to become a doctor. A man could study at home and be examined by a practicing physician who gave him a certificate if he passed his examination.

Many Jews were physicians to kings and nobles. Even the royal doctors remembered their duties as Jews and treated their own people. Poor Jews were not neglected. Doctors served them free of charge.

We leave Samuel at home with his teacher to go to the schoolhouse. Older pupils studied here. If the rabbi was well known, he might have students from far-away lands. In such a school the Talmud was taught and explained. The rabbi went over questions which he received from other cities and wrote responsa in answer. What to do when Jews were forcibly baptized and converted was a baffling question. Could a Jew return to Judaism after he was converted? The Halacha was called on to solve the problems which beset Jews living in lands sometimes friendly and sometimes hostile.

The rabbi felt a great responsibility when he answered these questions. He had to be learned, honest, and righteous. A great scholar was respected because he was the symbol of the Torah and its majesty. He was the example for his pupils to follow. Many letters have come down to us which show how rabbis loved their students and how students revered their teachers.

It would be interesting to follow an older student—we can call him Moses of Seville—as he hurried away from school. He might enter a modest home where he had a room. In the room were his books—books in Arabic as well as in Hebrew. A book was a precious thing in those days before printing was invented. The rabbis encouraged their students to lend one another books so all could benefit from their use. One well-known scholar wrote in a letter to his son:

"My son! Examine thy Hebrew books at every new moon. . . . Arrange thy library in fair order. . . . Never refuse to lend books to anyone who has not means to purchase books for

himself, but only act thus to those who can be trusted to return the volumes. . . . Cover the bookcases with rugs of fine quality; and preserve them from damp and mice, and from all manner of injury, for thy books are thy good treasure."

If Moses wrote poetry, as was the fashion in those days, he probably studied Hebrew grammar. It was a favorite study of those who loved the language, as poets do. Many poets were fine students of the Bible. Through their knowledge of Hebrew and its grammar they explained passages which were not clear because the Hebrew words had not been properly understood.

Perhaps Moses of Seville was hurrying to work. Down the narrow streets of the town he would run. Maybe he worked for a merchant who dealt with companies outside of Spain. Trade with North Africa, for example, was very common. He would deal not only with Jews—Christians, Moslems, and Jews did business together. Perhaps Moses wrote the letters for his employer, together with other duties. Sometimes it took a real mathematician to figure out the value of foreign money. If his employer was a "cambist" or money-changer, he had to recognize different coinage and know its value. In dealing with foreign countries, different moneys were used. Knowledge of foreign languages would also be useful.

If Moses lived with his father, he probably helped in a store or worked as a carpenter, a shoemaker, or tailor. Perhaps his father was a dealer in wine, for grapes were plentiful in the warm climate and wine was cheap and good. Maybe

he sold soap or candles, corn or wheat, or traded in leather, furs, or woolen cloth. One Jew was a lion-tamer in the palace —do you think Moses was his assistant?

A visitor to the town would notice the hospital near the synagogue. The hospital was supported by the wealthy men in town. Many of them set aside one-tenth of their earnings to give to those in need, for orphans and widows, and for the education of poor boys.

The great Jewish teacher of this period, Moses Maimonides, prepared a scale of charity. The first on the list is the finest kind of charity. The last is the least worthy. They are:

1. Helping a poor man by giving him a loan or taking him into business—that is, helping him to help himself.

2. Helping a poor man without knowing who is receiving the money, and not letting the poor man know who was his helper.

3. Giving to one whom you know, without letting him know who helped.

4. Giving, but letting the poor man know who helped.

5. Giving to a man who knows from whom the money comes, without being asked.

6. Giving after one is asked to help.

7. Giving in a kindly way, but not giving enough.

8. Giving, but in an unkindly manner.

One building was missing from the Jewish area. There was no jail. Though highwaymen roamed the roads, Jews were not among them. A theft or a robbery was almost unheard of. A man who committed a wrong was brought to the Jewish judges. If he was found guilty, he was fined or sometimes flogged.

The severest punishment was excommunication. If a man refused to obey the order of the court, he might be excommunicated. That meant he was no longer a member of the Jewish community. No one would have anything to do with him. No one would speak to him, or visit him, or do business with him. He was not permitted to enter the synagogue. He was alone—an outsider.

The rabbis and judges thought long and seriously before they decided on an excommunication. It was a dreadful punishment. It proved more powerful than the threats or terrors of a king or a caliph. Jews disciplined themselves by the strength of their religious laws and their respect for religious leaders.

One of the greatest burdens of the Jews in Spain and of other parts of Europe were the heavy taxes they had to pay the government. Taxes were levied to support the army and navy, and to pay for the wars which were so frequent. Taxes raised money for the royal family to pay for their huge estates, servants, travels, and extravagant clothing. Jews were called on to pay more than their just share of such taxes.

The tax officials were Jews who acted for the king. They tried to be fair. They were careful not to tax a widow or a newcomer to town. The rabbis and scholars were also free of taxes. That was because they served the community without pay and also was part of the honor which was due them and their position.

Before we leave this little town of long ago, we would like to know how the Jews spent their free time. What did they do for fun? Rich families had parties and were occasionally invited to state affairs and sports at the court. They wore fine clothes made of elegant fabrics and jewels on these occasions. In their own homes all Jews would celebrate the holidays and festivals. An engagement or a wedding was a feast day for everyone in town.

Jews learned one pastime from the Arabs which the rabbis frowned on. That was gambling. Many a scrap of paper has come down to us telling how Don Joseph or Don Emanuel promised faithfully never to gamble again.

What final picture of the town can we take with us? Let us imagine a last glimpse of Moses of Seville. He stands inside the courtyard of a house. In his hand is a tiny box. He has come to visit his betrothed, Beatrice, the daughter of Don Pedro and Donna Sarah. Through the windows, lighted by soft candles, we can see the young girl working on an embroidery loom. Her mother has a piece of sewing in her hands. Her father converses with another man—an open Hebrew book lying between them. Soon Moses will join them to give Beatrice the gift he has brought her.

So the tour comes to an end. It has shown us how Jews lived during the fortunate years which they had in Spain. Now let us learn about the great men, the fine ideals, and the excellent books which this period produced. It is a wonderful tale.

TALK OVER IN CLASS

Why was excommunication a terrible punishment? Why was it powerful?

A SPANISH EXHIBIT

At home, in school, and in the library, find as many objects as you can that have to do with Spain, or with Spanish-Jewish life. Bring them to your class. Clothing, coins, jewelry, pictures of public buildings and of synagogues are what you want. If you wish, you may copy pictures from the encyclopedia and make some objects from plasticine or clay. If you assemble a good exhibit, you might invite another class in for a visit.

23. THE SINGERS OF SPAIN

NOT FAR from the palace of the vizier or prime minister of the caliph in the city of Malaga, there was a tiny shop. In it a Jew named Samuel Ibn Nagdela carried on a humble business.

A slave woman from the vizier's palace often asked Samuel to write letters for her. She admired his beautiful handwriting and showed his letters to the vizier. The vizier called Samuel to his palace. He found, to his surprise, that the shopkeeper was a man who knew Hebrew and Arabic, Latin and Spanish, and also the language of the Berbers who were the rulers of the province. The vizier did not know that, in addition, Samuel was a scholar of the Talmud, a poet, a writer of thoughtful articles, and a composer of prayers for the synagogue.

Samuel became the vizier's secretary. The vizier asked him for advice and found it good. The caliph, in turn, was pleased with his vizier. But the day came when the vizier fell sick. He made a confession to his sovereign.

"The good advice I have given you," he said, "came from my secretary, the Jew, Samuel Ibn Nagdela. When I am gone, let him be your vizier."

The caliph listened to the words of his vizier. Samuel became adviser to the caliph. He carried on the tradition which was begun by Chasdai ibn Shaprut in Cordova, of deep Jewish learning and excellent statesmanship. Like Chasdai he was a pious Jew and served as rabbi and teacher. He is usually called Samuel ha-Nagid, or Samuel the Prince.

Samuel's duties at court were many and heavy, but he also found time to write books and articles about the Talmud, a Hebrew grammar, and hymns for the synagogue. He carried out one more important duty. He helped poets and writers with loans and gifts so they could write and study. Writers were often helped in this way in the Middle Ages. A man who followed this fine custom was called a "patron." Today a man who buys paintings, offers prizes for poetry, music, or medical research, or assists a university or museum, is called a "patron of the arts," or a "patron of learning."

For almost thirty years, until 1056 when he died, Samuel acted as prime minister. During this time and in the period which followed, the great Spanish writers gave us their poems and their songs, and wrote down their ideas about man and God.

Samuel was the patron of many poets. One of the best known of them was named Solomon Ibn Gabirol. He was one of the first Hebrew poets to write in rhyme. He could write rhymes as easily as you or I write prose. For example, he wanted to teach Hebrew grammar. He did not sit down and write a dry textbook. No. He wrote a long poem of four hundred verses, all in rhyme, telling the rules of grammar and why they should be studied.

Ibn Gabirol began to write poetry when he was very young. He wrote in Arabic and in Hebrew. Ibn Gabirol was poor and he wandered throughout Spain. His poetry is often sad, and he sometimes shows an angry mood. He was not a happy man.

In one poem he tells of his longing for the Messiah who will redeem Israel. He wrote:

Come up to me at early dawn,
Come up to me, for I am drawn
To thee by my own spirit's spell,
To see the sons of Israel.
For thee, O great one, I will spread
Within my court a golden bed,
And I will set a table there
And bread for thee I will prepare,
For thee my goblet I will fill
With juices that my vines distil.
And thou shalt drink to heart's delight
Of all my flavors day and night.
The joy in thee I will evince
With which a people greets its prince.
O son of Jesse, holy stem,
God's servant, born of Bethlehem!

Once he wrote, "I am the master, and song is a slave to me." That was the poet speaking from his heart.

Ibn Gabirol is remembered mainly for his great religious poems. He reached out to God for His help, to understand Him and to praise Him. The beautiful Hebrew of his poems and hymns found a place in the hearts of all who read them for hundreds of years. Those who read them in English and in other languages are still moved by their beauty. Many of them have been included in the prayer books, especially in the services for the High Holy Days.

Here is one of Ibn Gabirol's religious poems. It is called, "My Refuge," and tells how he thought of God as the One to whom he turned in time of trouble.

My Refuge

I have made Thee my refuge, in trembling and fear,
And when besieged, I have made Thee my tower.
When to left and to right I have sought for a helper,
I could look to no aid but Thy strength and Thy power.
More than all earthly treasure, I have made Thee my portion,
In all my cares, Thou fillest my days.
In the flood of Thy love I have gladness eternal,
And prayer is the time for singing Thy praise.

Gabirol was not only a poet. He was interested in the ideas of ancient Greek thinkers, and wanted to see how they would fit into the world of his day. One of his most important books had a curious history. He wrote this volume in Arabic, although it was known to Jews by its Hebrew name, *M'kor Chayim* or "The Source of Life." From its name, you can guess that this is not a book for you to read—not yet. You will have to wait a few years to understand Ibn Gabirol's ideas about God—the Source of life. However, the scholars of his time and later were very interested in this book. It was translated into Latin and for many years was studied by great Christian scholars. The name "M'kor Chayim" was forgotten. It was known only by its Latin name, *Fons Vitae.* Gabirol's own name had been written incorrectly and the author was supposed to be someone called Avicebrol.

About eight hundred years later, a scholar working in the National Library in Paris found part of the original Arabic of *M'kor Chayim,* and its Latin translation, *Fons Vitae.* He made the surprising discovery that they were the same book. Like a detective following a faint clue, he continued working and at last was able to prove his claim, that *Fons Vitae* by Avicebrol and *M'kor Chayim* by Ibn Gabirol were one and the same work. For eight hundred years it had been read and studied as the work of a Christian writer.

Just to list the names of the writers who were busy during this period would cover many a page. When Spanish Jews gathered together for an evening, one of them often brought along a new poem which had just appeared. The company might argue whether it was better than earlier poems and might compare it with the work of different writers. Perhaps a poet was present and he would be invited to read and recite his own poems. The heroes of the day were writers, teachers, and statesmen.

Hebrew learning was not neglected. The Talmud was studied in the academies which were found in every large city. A great interest was shown in the Bible and in the Hebrew language. Poets, grammarians and philosophers were all students of Jewish lore.

A writer who was not a poet but was very popular was named Bachya Ibn Pakuda. He worked on a serious book called, *The Duties of the Heart*. He was afraid that people were obeying Jewish laws and keeping Jewish customs without paying attention to their real meaning. He wanted the Torah to be followed because it brought people joy. Bachya followed in the footsteps of the Pharisees who found happiness in accepting and obeying the laws of the Torah.

Bachya said, "To serve God we must trust God. . . . Those who love God will do right without hope of reward, and will give up evil without fear of punishment."

Other writers like Bachya wrote books of advice and of good conduct. One man wrote a book of fables and maxims. Some of his wise sayings are very interesting. For example, he wrote, "Prefer the possession of one thing to the expectation of two" and "It is better to have simple contentment with freedom than luxury at someone else's table."

While Ibn Gabirol's songs were being sung all over Spain, another young poet began to write. His name was Yehuda Halevi. These poets are the two grand singers of the Golden Age.

It is good to know that Yehuda Halevi had a fortunate and happy life. He was born near Toledo and lived for many years in that pleasant medieval city. He traveled south to the all-Jewish city of Lucena for his Hebrew studies. That did not complete his education. To be a well-educated man of his day, he had to know something of mathematics, of astronomy, and of Arabic literature. He studied medicine, too, and earned his living as a physician.

A real poet does not sit down at a desk with a clean sheet of paper before him and say, "Now I will write a poem. What shall the subject be?" His poetry is part of his life and any

event can be the starting point of a poem. So it was with Yehuda Halevi. If a friend of his married, he wrote a poem in honor of the happy event. If he saw a lovely scene or a beautiful girl, it brought forth a poem. A sad occasion, like the death of a friend, was also remembered in poetry. He wrote for fun too. Here is a riddle of his in rhyme. See if you can guess the answer. (If not, look at the end of the chapter.)

What is it that's blind with an eye in its head,
And the children of men its use cannot spare,
Spends all its life in clothing mankind,
And always itself is naked and bare?

In all, Yehuda Halevi wrote more than eight hundred poems. Many of them remind us of the Psalms and were read in the synagogue. A person who knows the Bible well will recognize again and again references to the Bible and quotations from it, in Halevi's poems, for he knew the Bible and loved it.

One such poem is called, "O Lord, Where Shall I Find Thee?" It has been set to music and is often sung in the synagogue and at school assemblies.

O Lord, Where Shall I Find Thee?

O Lord, where shall I find Thee?
Hid is Thy lofty place;
And where shall I not find Thee,
Whose glory fills all space?
Who formed this world, abideth
Within man's soul alway;
Refuge for them that see Him,
Ransom for them that stray.

Who saith he hath not seen Thee,
Thy heavens refute his word;
Their hosts declare Thy glory,
Though never voice he heard.
That Thou, transcendent, holy,
Joyest in Thy creatures' praise,
And comest where men gather,
To glorify Thy ways.

Many wonderful poems of Yehuda Halevi have to do with the land of Israel. He longed to see Zion restored to the Jewish people. Like the prophets of old, he looked on Jerusalem as the center of the world. One of his most famous poems is called "Longing for Jerusalem." It says:

Oh, city of the world, with sacred spendor blest,
My spirit yearns to thee from out the far-off West,
A stream of love wells forth when I recall thy day,
Now is thy temple waste, thy glory passed away.
Had I an eagle's wings, straight would I fly to thee,
Moisten thy holy dust with wet cheeks streaming free.
Oh, how I long for thee! Although thy king has gone,
Although where balm once flowed, the serpent dwells alone.
Could I but kiss thy dust, I would not mind to die,
As sweet as honey then, thy soil and stones, thy sky.

Halevi, whose songs burst forth from his heart, had even more to give the world. He was a serious thinker on religion. He considered the religions of the world which he knew, Judaism, Christianity, and Islam, and compared them to one another. He also examined the ideas of philosophers, men who look to the mind to find answers to their questions.

Halevi wrote a book called, *The Kuzari*. He based his book on the story which Joseph, the king of the Khazars, wrote in his letter to Chasdai ibn Shaprut.

It all began with a dream. Bulan, the king of the Khazars, was troubled. He was a good man, but a pagan. He dreamed that an angel came to him and said, "You must find another way of serving God."

When the king awoke, he could not forget his dream. He summoned before him a philosopher and asked him what was his idea of God. His answer did not satisfy King Bulan. He ordered a Christian monk to visit him and asked him about his religion. The monk explained how Christians believed in one God and in the Bible, which they took over from the Jews. He added that they also believed in Jesus as the Messiah.

Bulan went further. He called on a Moslem to explain his religion. The Moslem told of Mohammed and his belief in one God, which he took from Judaism.

The king was astonished. He had not even thought of asking a Jew about his religion. And now both Christian and Moslem declared that their religion came from Judaism. He had always thought that Judaism was a despised and neglected faith.

Bulan called for a rabbi to answer his questions. After a long debate King Bulan was convinced that he preferred Judaism to other religions. He and his family and many Khazars adopted Judaism.

You can see that Halevi used the interesting story of the Khazars as a starting point to describe the excellence of Judaism. He discussed the ideas of the Greek sages as well as the religious ideas of his own time in this great book. *The Kuzari* became one of the important contributions of the Spanish era.

Yehuda Halevi wrote poem after poem about Jerusalem and the Holy Land. At last he came to an important decision. He would leave Spain to see for himself the land of his dreams. He began his travels. He moved triumphantly

through Spain. In every city he was met with honor. He set sail for Egypt. Through his poems we share the journey. On the ship he wrote a poem describing the sea and its perils. When he came to Alexandria, his admirers begged him to remain. The Jews of Cairo treated him royally. At some time on his travels he also visited Damascus and Tyre. Almost every stop was marked by a beautiful poem.

But he did not forget his resolve. At last he reached Jerusalem, and feasted his eyes on the places he had longed to see. His heart must have filled with joy at these moments.

Yehuda Halevi's story ends on a sad note. It is said that he died soon after his arrival in Jerusalem. Somehow we do not feel too sorrowful. We know he lived a happy life and brought beauty and song to the world. That is how we remember him and his glorious achievements.

In Jerusalem today, the streets of one section of the city are named for famous Spanish Jews. Yehuda Halevi Park is not far from Ibn Gabirol Avenue. Ibn Ezra Street and Al Charizi Road cross each other. Ben Maimon Street is named for Moses Maimonides, about whom you will hear in the next few pages. A walk through these streets is a reminder of the greatness of the days in Spain we are studying now.

(Answer to the riddle—a needle.)

QUESTIONS TO ANSWER

What subjects was a well-educated Spanish Jew expected to know?

What kind of poems did the famous Spanish poets write?

TALK OVER IN CLASS

One of your friends is finishing high school. His parents cannot afford to send him to college. Will he look for a patron to assist him? How can he find help in getting a college education?

How are writers and scientists helped in their work in our day?

Discuss the difference between receiving assistance from a patron, as was the case in the Middle Ages, and the way it is done today.

READ

Great Men in Israel by Weis, "The Jews and Their Arabian Neighbors," p. 66.

Watchmen of the Night by Kalisher, "The Star of Spain," p. 49.

Judah Halevi in Granada by Abraham Burstein.

LET'S SING

You will find Yehuda Halevi's poem, "Lord, Where Shall I Find Thee?" in the *Union Hymnal*. It is #21.

Other poems of Yehuda Halevi and Ibn Gabirol are in the Hymnal. Perhaps you can spend your next music period singing them.

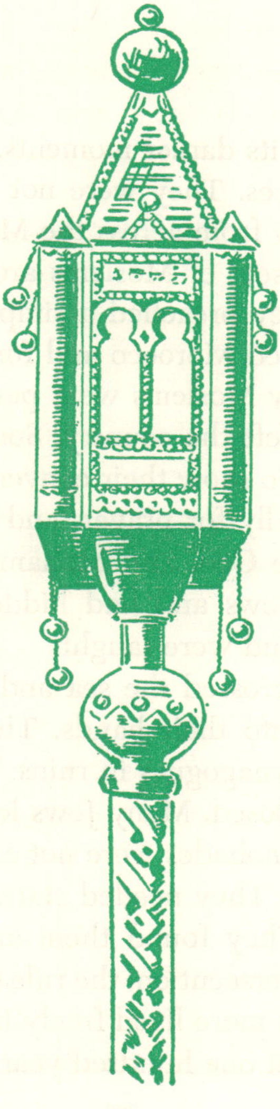

24. THE SECOND MOSES

SPAIN, TOO, had its darker moments. Andalusia was made up of many provinces. They were not united and could not withstand an enemy from across the Mediterranean Sea.

In Africa a new sect of Moslems arose. They were called the Almohades. They preached a simpler form of their religion. They conquered Morocco and forced their ideas on all its inhabitants. Only Moslems were permitted to live in Morocco. Many Jews left the country. Some Jews pretended to become Moslems. To show their conversion, they had to visit a mosque occasionally for prayer, and declare that they believed in Allah, one God, and Mohammed the prophet. Secretly, they were Jews and had hidden schools where the Bible and the Talmud were taught.

The Almohades crossed the sea and invaded Spain. Most of Andalusia fell into their hands. They tore through Cordova and left the synagogues in ruins. The schools in Seville and Lucena were closed. Many Jews left their homes.

However, the Almohades were not as well educated as the former Arab rulers. They needed statesmen, physicians, and men of learning. They found them among the Jews. After about ten years of persecution, the rule of the Almohades softened and Jews once more lived freely in their territory. Their rule lasted for about one hundred years.

Where could Jews go who fled from Andalusia? Some went to the north, where a number of large settlements had grown up under friendly Christian kings. Others went even farther, over the Pyrenees Mountains into France, and some crossed the Mediterranean.

That is how it happened that the greatest Jew of the Middle Ages, Moses ben Maimon, came to Egypt.

Moses' family left Cordova in 1148 when he was thirteen years old. At first they lived in various Spanish cities. Then they crossed the sea to North Africa and in time made their way down to Cairo.

Moses' father had been a judge in Cordova. He was a typical Jew of his time—well versed in general learning and a fine Jewish scholar as well. He began teaching his son at home, and found that the youngster was an amazing student. Years of wandering did not keep Moses from acquiring a great store of knowledge. He mastered the Bible and the Talmud, and the writings of later Jewish sages. He became familiar with the work of ancient Greek thinkers and of Arabic writers. In between he studied medicine. Later, he earned his living as a physician.

Moses ben Maimon is usually called by the Greek form of his name—Maimonides. In Hebrew his name is written in a kind of shorthand, using the initials which compose it—Rabbi Moses ben Maimon or "RaMBaM." We will come across contractions like this more than once.

Maimonides showed early that he was to be a leader in Jewry. He became known through books which he wrote while he was still a young man. His books were about the Mishnah and the Talmud and about logic, the science which explains the principles of clear thinking.

While the Maimon family lived in Morocco, the burning question of the day was: "Is it right for Jews even to pretend to be Moslems? Do they remain Jews if they practice their religion in secret?"

Moses wrote a letter to the Jews of Morocco which went to the heart of the matter. He analyzed their situation carefully. They had not been asked to give up their religion or to sin against it. They were ordered only to repeat the statement about Allah and Mohammed. Maimonides declared that if they did not believe in these words, they meant nothing. Jews who repeated them could consider themselves Jews and carry on their own religion in secret. But Maimonides knew how hard such a course of action could be. He advised the Jews to leave Morocco if they could and find a new home where they could be free and loyal to their own faith.

These were dangerous words. The Maimon family had to flee from Morocco. They would have liked to settle in Palestine, which they visited. But the Jews there were few in number and scattered. Maimonides looked for a community to live in where there were other scholars with whom he could discuss the problems of the day. He hoped to have students, too, with whom he could delve into the great works of Jewish tradition.

In Cairo, Maimonides and his family found what they

wanted. The Jews there were free and had their own governor, called the Nagid. The Sultan, Saladin, was a wise ruler, friendly to scholars and fair to men of other religions.

Maimonides became the physician to the vizier and to the family of the caliph. He also became the great Jew of his day. He was doctor, nasi, rabbi, and gaon, all rolled into one.

On one point Rambam was very firm. He felt that no rabbi should be paid for his duties. His service to his fellow Jews should be a labor of love, while he earned his living in some other way. Maimonides worked from early morn until late at night, as physician, as teacher and rabbi, and as a writer. Perhaps he did not realize how unusual he was. Other men could not hope to do what he did.

In a letter to one of his pupils he wrote:

"It is better for you to earn a drachma as wages for the work of a weaver, tailor or carpenter, than to be dependent on others. My opinion is that you should pay full attention to your trade or medical practice and at the same time continue the study of the Torah. But whatever you choose as your occupation, may the Lord guide you to find the right way."

Rambam practiced what he preached. He described his day in a famous letter to a French scholar who wished to come to visit him. He told him not to come for he was too busy to spend time with him. He wrote:

"I dwell at Fostat and the Sultan resides at Cairo. These two places are about three miles distant from each other. My duties to the Sultan are very heavy. I am obliged to visit him every day and when he or any of his children are indisposed, I dare not leave Cairo but must stay during the greater part of the day in the palace. . . . Hence, as a rule, I go to Cairo very early in the day, and even if nothing unusual happens, I do not return to Fostat until the afternoon. Then I am

nearly dying with hunger. . . . I find the antechambers filled with people, both Jews and Gentile, noble and common people, who await the time of my return.

"I partake of some slight refreshment, the only meal I take in the twenty-four hours. Then I go forth to attend to my patients. . . . Patients go in and out until nightfall, and sometimes even until two hours or more in the night. . . .

"On the Sabbath, the whole congregation, or at least the majority of the members, come to me after the morning service, when I instruct them . . . we study together until noon. In the afternoon some of them return, and read with me the afternoon service until evening prayers. . . . I have related to you only a part of what you would see if you were to visit me. . . .

"May your happiness, my son and pupil, increase, and help be granted to our afflicted people."

Jewish eyes were turned to Cairo. From near and far came letters and requests. Maimonides answered them all, writing most of the letters himself. His letters show not only great wisdom, they reveal a kind and gentle heart. When a convert asked if he might say, "Our God, and God of our Fathers," in the same way as one who was born a Jew, Maimonides answered, "Yes, you too are the son of Abraham, our father."

The Jews of Yemen were in trouble. They were ordered to accept Islam. The Yemenite Jews were not men of learning and their leaders feared that in time their pretense of being Mohammedans would become real. A false Messiah appeared who filled the people with vain hopes. The Jews of Yemen wrote to Maimonides asking for advice.

Maimonides wrote them a long, wise letter which gave them courage to bear their troubles. They did not follow the false Messiah. In time the government changed and their persecution stopped.

Maimonides' letters are very important. They throw light on how Jews were living and what they were doing in many parts of the world. Many of his letters and fragments of his writings were saved by being hidden away for many years. Because Jews always looked on Hebrew as a holy tongue, they would not throw away or destroy anything written in Hebrew. A worn-out Torah scroll, for example, was reverently buried. But Jewish custom went even further. Leaves torn from books, bits of parchment, letters, bills, synagogue records—practically everything written in Hebrew was saved. Maimonides' synagogue in Cairo became the storehouse for thousands of such odds and ends which came from other places as well as from Cairo. A storehouse of this kind is called

"Genizah"—a hiding place. The storeroom of the Cairo synagogue is called "The Genizah," that is, *the* hiding place.

You remember that Dr. Schechter * came to Cairo seeking the original of *The Wisdom of Ben Sira.* He found what he sought in the Genizah together with many other documents and papers which shed light on bygone days. Unknowingly, the Jews of the Middle Ages left a valuable treasure for the future in Cairo. Many of Maimonides' writings remained in the genizah waiting to be discovered years later.

Maimonides' letters were only a tiny part of his work. He wrote three great books of Jewish wisdom. The first was called *The Light* and was written in Arabic. It was an explanation of the Mishnah. In *The Light* Maimonides did something which had never been done before. He prepared a list of thirteen statements or principles of Judaism, which he declared every Jew must believe. The Middle Ages was a time of strict belief and the Jews gratefully turned to Maimonides for leadership and authority.

Rambam then turned his attention to the Talmud. He

* See page 101.

prepared a Code or list of all the laws in the Talmud. You remember how the Tannaim and the Amoraim would often leave the main thread of discussion and bring in other subjects. Halacha and Agaddah were mingled in page after page. Maimonides collected all the laws from the Bible and the Talmud. Everything was arranged systematically. The laws, how they came to be, the decisions of the geonim and other scholars, and his own opinions are put down in good order. The student of the Talmud found Maimonides' Code of untold value. It was called the "'Mishneh Torah" or "The Torah Repeated."

The Mishneh Torah has another name which is more meaningful and more poetic. It is "Yad Hachazakah," or "The Mighty Hand." This comes from the last verse of the Book of Deuteronomy and describes the work which Moses the Lawgiver did for Israel. How appropriate that the work of the second Moses should have this name! Moses Maimonides worked ten years on "The Mighty Hand." It is written in the fine Hebrew style of the Mishnah, the heritage of Judah ha-Nasi.

Somehow, in between those busy days and nights, Rambam found time for one more great book. This too has a striking name. It is called, *Moreh N'vuchim,* or *The Guide of the Perplexed.* It was written for students and teachers. Maimonides did not think the ordinary man would be interested or would understand his ideas on religion and philosophy. He was mistaken. The book became very popular, and was read and studied far and wide. Maimonides asked if a man could be a good Jew, believing in God, and yet find truth in the books of other peoples. Many more problems, which troubled not only Jews but all religious thinkers, were discussed in "The Guide." Perhaps when you are grown up you will take a course on "The Guide of the Perplexed." It was written originally in Arabic and later translated into many other languages and has been studied by men of all faiths.

The great teacher and lover of his people died in 1204. His death closed an epoch in Jewish history. Truly it could be said, "From Moses unto Moses, there was none like Moses."

The Golden Age came to an end. Its poets had sung their verses and their poems; its statesmen had sat near the thrones of kings; its thinkers had explained the lofty ideas of sages and scholars. But the Golden Age lived on in Jewish schools and homes. When the pages of history grew darker, its proud memories brought strength and hope.

OLD AND NEW

What do the initials RMBM stand for?

What do the initials UNESCO stand for?

Which came first?

Explain the sentence, "Jews in many lands looked to Cairo for guidance."

Explain the sentence, "From Moses unto Moses, there was none like Moses."

Make a list of the many different kinds of work which Maimonides did. Arrange them in the order of their importance.

READ

The Great March, Book I, by Lurie, "Tables Turned," p. 175.

The Boy of Cordova by Abraham Burstein.

Unit 8

Under Christian Rule

Jewish life developed differently as Jews traveled to new lands where they had to adapt to varying conditions. We make a big jump now, to northern France and to Germany, to the pleasant area of southern France called the Provence Region, and down across the Pyrenees into the northern part of Spain.

These three regions had one thing in common. Their rulers were Christian and the Catholic church had its representatives in all their cities.

Two centuries of quiet living were followed by a period of terror. Rulers who had been friends and protectors joined in attacking loyal subjects.

Could there be light in such a period of alarm and anxiety?

Could there be light at a time when no one knew what the morrow would bring?

High courage—intense study—the helping hand—the sturdy heart—were the lights that played among the shadows.

Which Jews showed these wonderful qualities? How did they face their misfortunes?

The Crusaders

25. ON BOTH SIDES OF THE RHINE

IF WE wished to describe the life of the Jews of Christian Europe in one word, that word would be "unstable." The dictionary says that means, "subject to sudden change."

Europe itself was not a stable place. It was divided into many small provinces, each ruled by a king or a noble. The nobles vied with one another for power. The officials of the church, clergymen and bishops, disputed with the king and his courtiers. The pope in Rome wanted to be the supreme ruler, holding sway over kings, nobles, and churchmen. A sudden change was not unusual for anyone.

Jewish life followed a basic pattern. Quiet years alternated with periods of disturbance. The Jews came to France in the early days of Roman rule and lived peacefully among their Christian neighbors. They carried on the usual pursuits of men of their time and place. Among farmers, they farmed. In towns they were merchants and artisans.

This quiet existence could be changed by a ruling of the Church. The ruling might order Christians to stay away from Jews. It might say that Jews were not permitted to engage in certain occupations. It might even force them to leave a place for a while.

Sometimes the king and the churchmen did not agree. A wise ruler would refuse to listen to the bishop. A kind priest would protect the Jews in his parish. On the other hand, kings and bishops sometimes acted together and enforced harsh laws. On the seesaw of the struggle for power, the fortunes of the Jews rose and fell.

With this general picture in mind, let us turn to the Jews of France and Germany living near the Rhine River. Their history is not as showy or spectacular as the story of the Jews of Andalusia. Except in unusual cases, they were not advisers to kings. Nor did poets or scientists come from their midst. Their scholars were men of the Torah, students of the Bible and the Talmud. They lived quietly together, industrious and thrifty, following their religion and observing the laws of the land.

Their communities were rather small. Fifty or sixty families made up a settlement and a town with two hundred families was considered large. Everyone in these towns knew one another and shared joys and sorrows.

The synagogue was their place of worship, their meeting hall, and their house of study. A stranger in town came to the synagogue. Perhaps he was a teacher on his way to a new post, or an artisan seeking a place to settle with his family. A traveler on his way to the Holy Land would pause to rest. A special welcome awaited him.

Each town and village had its school as well as its synagogue. The rabbi or a special teacher taught the boys in the school, and their fathers gathered in the synagogue to read and to study the Torah. The rabbi, like those in other countries, had another occupation. He may have had a tiny store or followed a humble craft like tailoring or cobbling. Sometimes he was a copier of Hebrew books.

The home life of the Jews in the Rhineland was pleasant and comfortable. They were pious Jews who enjoyed the ceremonies of every-day life, the rest of the Sabbath day, and the pleasure of the holidays and festivals.

In 768 the countries of France and Germany and part of Italy were united under a fine ruler named King Charlemagne, which is the French way of saying Charles the Great. He created a stable government. He was a great ruler in many ways. He held together a large empire which prospered under his rule.

A large united territory means opportunity for trading, and the Jews used it well. They traded in spices and silks, furs and metals. Goods came in from the East and were sold or exchanged for merchandise made in the West.

In many ways, Jews were especially well suited for trading. When they traveled from city to city and from country to country they counted on help from their fellow Jews. In a strange town, Jews went to the synagogue for information and help. Often they had friends or relatives in distant lands. Their common language, Hebrew, was not only a language of prayer. It helped in business too.

King Charlemagne once sent a delegation of three men to

the caliph at Bagdad. One of them was Isaac, a Jew. The hardships of travel proved too much for two of the ambassadors. But Isaac arrived safely at the court of the caliph where he represented his royal master. Then he made the long trek back to France to report on his mission to Charlemagne. No doubt Isaac was helped on his way by Jewish friends as he passed from town to town.

King Charlemagne did not pay attention to laws against Jews passed by the Church. He did not separate Jews from the rest of his subjects. If they were good and faithful citizens, he took care of them. During his reign, new synagogues were built. Among those who came to listen to the rabbis were a number of Christians who enjoyed the explanations of the Jewish teachers. Nevertheless, some church laws against Jews were generally observed.

Some bishops did not like to see Christians become friendly with Jews. Christians were forbidden to eat in Jewish homes and were warned not to marry Jews. Clergymen were always concerned about Christians who might be slaves or servants to Jews, and forbade any Christian to work for a Jew. Servants who worked for Jews sometimes preferred their employers' religion to their own. The simplest solution to this problem in the eyes of hostile churchmen was to forbid Christians to work for Jews. This was one of the reasons that Jews gradually gave up farming. In those days, only human hands could do the farmer's work. Tractors and threshers were not even dreamed about. A farmer could not care for large fields with only his family to help.

But the king was watchful. Laws decreed by the pope or by the councils of the church had to have his approval. Charlemagne's son, King Louis, followed his father's example of fairness and justice. A council of bishops asked him to take some privileges away from the Jews in his land. He would not agree. He said, "The law of God orders me to protect my subjects who share my belief, but it does not forbid me to be unjust to those who differ from me."

To defy the Church like that was the act of an honest and brave man. Even a king could not always resist when bishops opposed him.

The kingdom broke up at about the year 1000. The Jews were no longer protected by one ruler who commanded a large area. In his place, kings, dukes, and lords ruled smaller territories. Each Jewish settlement had its own individual problem. A bishop or priest was often able to influence a less important noble. On the other hand, a greedy ruler would accept a gift in exchange for a favor.

The change in rulers took place at about the time when Jewish life was breaking up in the East and growing strong in the West. You remember that Moses ben Chanoch came to Spain in 965. Cordova became a center of learning. France and Germany shared with Spain in the transfer of Jewish learning from Babylonia.

The first of the great teachers of the Rhineland studied in France but lived and taught in Mayence, Germany. His name was Rabbi Gershom. When he became famous he was called "Rabbenu Gershom" or "Our Teacher Gershom." His pupils and admirers gave him another name. It was "M'or Hagola," or "The Light of the Exile."

Rabbenu Gershom was the head of a large Talmudic academy. Students came to him from France, Germany, and from Italy. From his school they went forth to teach and to act as rabbis.

Do you remember how Rabbi Samuel in Nehardea made a ruling which became part of Jewish law forever after? In the same way, Rabbenu Gershom, with the help of a group of scholars whom he called together, made some important rulings. They were necessary because of the changes which had taken place in the five hundred years which had passed since the Talmud was written down.

The first rule stated that no Jew could have more than one wife. The Talmud had no law about this, and since it was permitted by the Bible, a man would occasionally marry more than one wife. The second regulation said that no man could divorce his wife unless she agreed to the divorce.

The third ruling was quite different. It was about letters and travelers. Travelers often acted as postmen. They took letters with them from one place to another. Some of them may have been tempted to open a letter to read it. Rabbi Gershom declared that a letter is a private affair. Only the sender and the one who is to receive it should know its contents. One who carried a letter was forbidden to open it or to read it.

The laws of Rabbenu Gershom went out to the Jews of Europe. Those who did not obey them were to be punished by excommunication.

The fear of excommunication was not the only reason why these laws were followed. The first reason was that they were good and necessary. The second reason was the place of respect and honor which Rabbenu Gershom had among the Jews of Europe. He had no police or army to enforce his laws. But the words of "The Light of the Exile" were enough. From that time forth, European Jews followed the regulations of Rabbenu Gershom.

It is sad to know that Rabbenu Gershom lived to see the Jews of Mayence in trouble. The German emperor was very angry because a church official had become a Jew. His conversion was the signal for a series of laws against Jews which ended in a stern decree: "Become a Christian or leave the land!"

Some Jews were baptized. They became Christians. Others who would not falter had to leave their homes. Later, a huge bribe changed the hearts of the officials and Jews returned to Mayence.

What about those families who had accepted Christianity and then wished to return to their former religion? Rabbenu Gershom gave a clear answer. They were to be taken back without question into the congregation. No one was to remind them of what they had done at a time of despair.

The teachers at Mayence continued their work after Rabbenu Gershom died. One of their pupils was a young man named Solomon, the son of Isaac. He came from the other side of the Rhine, from Troyes, in France.

We do not know very much about Solomon's early life. He came from a family of scholars. He could not have had very much money, for once he wrote that while he studied, he traveled about, "in want of food and in ragged clothes." But food was not important to the young student. More important was his desire to listen to rabbis and teachers in different towns.

Rabbi Solomon, the son of Isaac, was too long a name. His pupils used his initials, RaShI, to make a shorter name, and as Rashi he is known to this day.

Rashi was invited to be the rabbi of Troyes. He settled down in the town of his birth in about 1065. Troyes was a busy city but its fame among Jews does not rest on its commerce. It is remembered as the city of Rashi, famous teacher, wise rabbi, and upright man. Many a trader, finishing his work at the fair, would remain in Troyes for an extra day or

two to visit Rashi's school and to hear him speak
Rashi kept a vineyard and earned his living tendi
Pupils came to Rashi while he was still a young
went over the Talmud with them, he wrote in h
the explanations which he gave them of difficult points. Slowly the notes grew in size. At last he gathered them into a "Commentary" or book of explanations. His explanations were good, clear and easy to understand. From his time on, the Talmud was always studied together with Rashi's Commentary. In fact, after printing was invented every copy of the Talmud contained Rashi's explanations right next to the Mishnah and the Gemara.

Rashi also kept in mind the ordinary man. He knew that not everyone could become a student of the Talmud. But practically every man of his day knew enough Hebrew to read the Bible. He wrote a commentary on the Bible, too.

Sometimes even Rashi was not sure of the meaning of a verse or passage. He was not ashamed to say so. He wrote, "I do not know" or "I am not sure."

Rashi's commentary on the Bible became very popular. In towns and hamlets, Jews read it eagerly. The beauty and wisdom of the Holy Scriptures became clear. A boy's first subject after he could read Hebrew was "Chumosh—the Five Books of Moses." Then he began the study of "Rashi."

The quiet days of Rashi's life were disturbed a few years before his death. The Jews of Germany and France lived through a period of suffering and persecution which was different from any known before in Jewish life. These terrible years began when the Christian world set out on a series of holy wars, known as Crusades. You will hear of them later.

Before we come to them, let us see how the Jews in the Provence and in northern Spain were faring.

QUESTIONS TO ANSWER

Who were well-known teachers of the Rhineland?

For what is each one best remembered?

In what ways was a knowledge of Hebrew useful to a Jew of Europe?

TALK OVER IN CLASS

What do you think of Rabbenu Gershom's ruling about Jews who were forcibly converted? Do you agree that they should have been permitted to return to Judaism? What did other rabbis have to say about this problem?

READ

Great Men in Israel by Weis, "Why a Rich Man Went Hungry," p. 84; "The Rabbi and the Bishop," p. 87.

The Boy Called Rashi by Abraham Burstein.

READINGS FOR TEACHERS

Unit 8 (*CHAPTERS 25–28*)

A History of the Jews, Book III, by Grayzel, Chaps. I, II.

A History of the Jewish People by Margolis and Marx, Chaps. L, LV.

Great Jewish Books by Caplan and Ribalov, Biographical Sketch of Rashi, p. 114.

26. TRANSLATORS AND TRAVELERS

A GOOD name for the Jews of southern France would be the "in-betweeners." Geographically, they were settled in between France and Germany to the north, and Spain to the south. Religiously, they were "in-between." Their Christian neighbors were far more liberal than the Christians in the north of France. Their bishops and priests were interested in the ideas of Judaism and saw no harm in free discussions between Christians and Jews.

Jewish settlements, large and small, dotted this pleasant countryside. In the smaller villages, Jews owned vineyards and farms. Many Jewish physicians were trained in a college in the city of Montpellier and we are told that Jews were among the teachers in the medical school. In the large city of Marseilles, which was a shipping center, they engaged in navigation and probably sent ships down the coast of Spain to Italy and to North Africa. From these points, traders made overland journeys eastward for spices and fine furs. Homeward bound, the ship might pick up travelers from foreign points. When the Jews fled from Cordova and Granada some of them may well have embarked on the ships of the Jews of Marseilles for safety and a welcome in southern France.

The Jews of southern France were "in-betweeners" in another way. They were the intermediaries who brought the poetry and wisdom of the Golden Age to the rest of Europe. They translated the great works of Spanish Jews from Arabic into Hebrew. A vast Hebrew reading public, which stretched over Central Europe and across the Channel to England, was ready for these books.

The Arabic writings of Ibn Gabirol, Yehuda Halevi, and Saadiah Gaon became known to men who could not have read their books in the original. Translations of Maimonides' works were eagerly awaited in far-off lands.

Two families who settled in Narbonne and in Lunel were the best-known translators. They were the Kimchi family and

the Ibn Tibbons. Do you remember the advice about the care of books which was quoted in an earlier chapter? It was part of a letter written by Judah Ibn Tibbon to his son Samuel. Both Judah and Samuel became famous as translators. Samuel was the translator of Maimonides. He wrote to Rambam and in reply received the famous letter describing his day. In addition Maimonides gave him good advice on translations. He said, "The translator should try to grasp the sense of the passage thoroughly, and then state the author's meaning correctly in the other language. This cannot be done without changing the order of words if necessary, or putting many words for one, so that the subject will be perfectly understood in the language into which he translates. . . ."

Up to the beginning of the thirteenth century, southern France was a region of peace and plenty—a bridge between north and south, east and west.

Let us cross over the Pyrenees now and stay for a while in the northern part of Spain. Andalusia in the south was but a tiny area in the large Spanish peninsula. But Jews also lived in the rest of Spain under a Christian king, Alphonso, who united most of northern Spain. He was the first Christian king to challenge Mohammedan rule.

Jews were as important in his reign as they had been in southern Spain. They were the king's advisers and he sent them on diplomatic missions. They fought under his banner. His reign was marked by the privileges and equality which Jews shared with Christians.

The news of King Alphonso's unusual treatment of Jews came to the ears of the pope. He wrote a strong letter to the king saying, "You must not permit Jews to rule over Christians." But Alphonso needed the help of Jews and paid no attention to the instructions of the pope.

Moslem weakness in Spain began when the city of Toledo fell to the Christians in 1085. Years of fighting between Christian and Moslem rulers followed. At length only Granada was held by Moslems. Many years later that too was taken from them. The Moslems then left Spain. The beautiful palace in

Granada, the Alhambra, is a reminder of their magnificent days. One of our best-known American writers, Washington Irving, lived in Granada for many years, and wrote a book about the fabulously beautiful palace of the caliphs.

In 1148, when the Almohades descended upon Cordova and Jews fled from that city, many of them came up to Toledo. Toledo took the place of Cordova. It had fine synagogues and schools. Barcelona and Saragossa were other cities where Jews lived quietly. They did not match in scholarship, poetry, or science the fine figures of Cordova and Malaga, but among them were scientists, philosophers, teachers, and poets.

A good picture of how Jews were living in far-away lands came from a man who did not expect his name to be remembered in the company of the great men of his day. His name was Benjamin and he came from the city of Tudela in northwestern Spain. Benjamin of Tudela was a merchant and he traveled from his native land to almost every part of the

world where Jews lived. He was away from Spain for thirteen years.

A traveler in the twelfth century did not set out lightly on a journey. His trip could not be arranged by a travel agency. Roads were bad and robbers often lay in wait for coaches and lonely horsemen. Inns were rude shelters. Ships were not built with water-tight compartments. Their captains had only crude instruments to help them chart the stars to guide them on their course. Benjamin's long journey was an unusual achievement.

It would be a good idea to follow Benjamin's route on the map. He went from Spain to southern France and then to Italy. From Italy he visited Greece, Syria, Palestine and Babylonia, and the city of Bagdad. On the way home he saw Yemen and Egypt. He returned to Spain from Sicily.

During his travels, Benjamin kept a diary, and this is his gift to everyone who is interested in the story of the Jewish people. He mentioned the names of a hundred different places, some forgotten, some unknown. He was a census taker, and kept a record of the number of Jews who lived in each place he visited. He noted the occupations of Jews: silk weavers in Greece, dyers in Palestine, glassmakers and shipowners in Syria. He found small colonies of Jews scattered over Palestine.

Benjamin remained for a while in Bagdad where an exilarch appointed by the caliph once more headed the community. One of the most striking of Benjamin's tales was about a false Messiah who appeared to the Jews of this area. North of Bagdad, in the city of Amadia, lived a young man named David Alroy. He was a fine scholar of the Bible and the Talmud and was much admired because of his knowledge. David Alroy declared that God had appointed him to deliver the

Jews from Moslem rule, and to lead them back to Jerusalem. He appeared before the sultan claiming to be the Messiah. Without much ado, the sultan cast him into prison, but he escaped from it by "magic." No doubt the magic was bachsheesh, a bribe.

A large number of Jews believed in David Alroy. They were ready to fight their way to Jerusalem. But David Alroy's claims came to naught, and the Jews had to return to their homes, poorer and sadder.

A very different kind of traveler from Benjamin of Tudela was Abraham Ibn Ezra of Toledo. Although he came from an illustrious and wealthy family, he himself was always poor. Somehow he could not make a living, try as he would. Once he wrote about himself:

> If I sold shrouds, no one would die,
> If I sold lamps, then in the sky
> The sun for spite,
> Would shine at night.

When he found that he could not settle down to a life of comfort, he began to travel. Clever and witty, a scholar of note, he was sure of a welcome wherever he went. He journeyed to Egypt, Palestine, and as far off as Bagdad. Homeward bound, he lived for a while in Rome.

For a few years he remained in Italy. While there, he began to work on a number of Bible commentaries. With a clear and understanding mind, he wrote brilliant explanations of Koheleth, the Song of Songs, Ruth, Esther, and Lamentations. He followed this work with a commentary on the Five Books of Moses.

The Jews of Italy treated Ibn Ezra with warmth and affection. He excited them and challenged them to study. Compared to this striking Spanish scholar, their own teachers were dull, following old ideas. He had many pupils and encouraged them to continue studying.

Restless as ever, Ibn Ezra sailed to southern France, where he was greatly admired. Then he went on to England. All the while he continued writing. He completed books explaining the Prophets and the Book of Daniel. He was happy in England. He found a patron in London who helped him and students who listened eagerly to his words. But the urge to wander never left him and off he went again, wandering almost to the day of his death.

Ibn Ezra worked until he was a very old man. His books on the Bible are only part of his work. He wrote poetry, books on Hebrew grammar, on astronomy and on mathematics. He was one of the Spanish Jews of later days who was as many-sided as the Jews of Andalusia.

Once Ibn Ezra wrote of his experience with a rich man. He said:

> I come in the morn
> To the house of the nobly born,
> They say he rode away.
> I come again at the end of the day,
> But now he is at rest.
> He either sleeps or rides afar—
> Woe to the man who was born without a star.

In this verse, Abraham Ibn Ezra refers to himself as a man born without a star, that is, a lucky star. Perhaps he was unsuccessful in the eyes of those who believe wealth is the sign of success. What do you think?

While Ibn Ezra traveled from land to land, Spanish Jews were still able to give a good account of themselves. Some of them rose high in the esteem of their rulers. The tradition of helping scholars and poets was carried on. Jewish learning went on in every city.

But a great change was to come to the Jews of Europe. It came slowly to Spain, and more quickly and sharply to the Jews of the Rhineland.

The Middle Ages became the Dark Ages. The hostile Christian church grew stronger than ever before. From king to peasant, every man obeyed its demands. The Jews were not the only ones who suffered in those days, but their trials were the hardest and the longest. The homes of Rabbenu Gershom and of Rashi were the first to feel the effects of Chri: power.

QUESTIONS TO ANSWER

Where did the Ibn Tibbon family and the Kimchi family live?
What important task did they perform?
How did their work help to unite Jews in different lands?
What advice did Maimonides give to his translators?
What do we learn from Jewish travelers of long ago?
Which city took the place of Cordova when Jews fled northwest?
Was it under Moslem or Christian rule at that time?

READ

Great Men in Israel by Weis, "The Globe-Trotter," p. 74.
The Great March, Book I, by Lurie, "An Angel Did It," p. 161.

27. THE TERRIBLE CRUSADES

SOME PEOPLE might say, "Let us skip over the next part of our history quickly. It is full of sorrow and hardship." Rabbis and teachers have talked this over many times. They agree that history is an honest record of events. It must tell of troubled times as well as days of gladness.

The period which began at about 1100 was indeed a dark era. It changed the situation of Jews in almost every country. Well-established communities disappeared. Families became homeless. Well-to-do men lost their wealth. Friends turned into foes.

It seems like a miracle that Jewish life continued at all. The reason was clear. The Jews fought back. When they could, they fought with swords and spears. These were only temporary aids. For their enemies usually had more and better weapons, and greater numbers.

The Jews fought with weapons of the mind and heart. Strength and consolation came from the pages of the Bible and the words of teachers and sages. Rabbis came together to make rules to meet new problems which had to be solved. A remarkable feeling of unity made every Jew "his brother's keeper," to help and to sustain him.

In 1095, a church council was held in southeastern France. At this meeting, the pope called on the Christians of the world to engage in a holy war. The aim of the war was to recapture Jerusalem from the Turks who held it at that time. The Christians regarded Jerusalem as their holy city, and wanted it to be in their hands.

Thus began the Crusades.

In the spring of 1096, a mixed horde of thousands of men started marching to Palestine. Their route led from France into Germany. At their head was Peter the Hermit preaching at every stop for more Crusaders to join his ranks. The First Crusade was made up of some loyal Christians moved by the words of their leaders. The greater number of Crusaders were peasants who saw the chance to free themselves from their hated feudal lords and adventurers looking for easy spoil. To them the holy war was a great spree. They had two objects. One was to get booty. The other was to fulfill the words of their leader—to kill a non-believer.

At first "non-believer" meant a Moslem. Then a different meaning spread. The Jews were non-believers, too. In addition, the Jews were near at hand. Why wait until the Crusaders reached Jerusalem? Both aims could be achieved on the way.

French Jews sent warnings across the Rhine. The Jews of Germany hardly believed them. For years they had been living peacefully in sleepy German towns. They looked to the emperor of Germany and to the bishops of their towns for protection. The emperor was away in Italy. A few stout-hearted bishops who believed that being a Christian meant to behave righteously protected the Jews in their districts. They took Jews into their castles and confronted the invaders with

armed men. But others demanded baptism as the price of safety. Some nobles and churchmen agreed to hand the Jews over to the mobs and greedily took a share of the booty.

The story was repeated in town after town. The Jews were easily found. Their synagogue marked the center of their settlement. Usually it went up in flames. Then nearby homes were broken into and looted. Anything of value was stolen. Jews were killed wherever they were found. Even when they were sheltered by Christian neighbors, with whom they had been friends for years, or in the castle of an honest bishop or noble, they were not always safe. In some towns, after the Crusaders marched through, not a Jew was left alive.

Sometimes the Crusaders were satisfied with conversion. At the point of a sword, thousands of Jews accepted Christianity.

Many stories of heroism come from these days. Jews courageously defended themselves and their families. When overwhelming numbers attacked them, they did not wait. Death at their own hands with the rabbi's blessing was preferred to the violence of a mob.

From Germany the Crusaders went eastward to Bohemia, the country which is now Czechoslovakia. The old community of Prague was destroyed, together with many other settlements.

The First Crusade would have been a sorry failure if it had depended on the undisciplined mob which raged through Europe, bent more on thievery and destruction than on a holy cause. But they were joined by a host of soldiers commanded by trained officers. This army crossed over from Constantinople and in July, 1099, captured Jerusalem.

The Crusaders did not follow the good example of the Moslem conquerors years before. At that time Jews and Christians were permitted to remain in the Holy Land. The Crusaders drove out or killed every Jew and every Moslem in Jerusalem.

In Central Europe, Jews returned to broken homes and burned synagogues. In some cases there were no Jews to return. The German emperor was ashamed of the ruin and havoc wrought by the Crusaders. He declared that all Jews who were forcibly baptized could return to their faith. He ordered their property returned to them whenever possible.

The Second and then the Third Crusade followed. A hundred years passed. The Crusaders did not accomplish their purpose, for Saladin, the sultan whom Maimonides served, defeated them in 1187. Jerusalem was once more in Moslem hands. Saladin generously permitted the Christians to hold on to one church in the Holy City. Scattered Jews returned to Jerusalem and other parts of Palestine.

The Crusades changed the conditions of Jewish life in Central Europe. In the first place, thousands were killed. Many others were converted. The position of the Jews who were left was unstable. It depended on the good will of the king or of the ruler of the district. When danger threatened he might offer protection, but always at a price.

The Jews lost the freedom they had enjoyed. They were considered "royal servants." Their property was practically in the hands of their ruler. When he needed money, he called on them for a huge tax. In addition, he could "sell" the Jews of a city or district to another ruler. Then the taxes of the Jews went to the new prince. It did not take long for well-to-do communities to become poverty-stricken.

Foreign and local trading had been Jewish occupations for hundreds of years. But men who are fleeing for their lives cannot engage in business. The Crusaders opened the way for Christian traders to follow to other lands. By the time the Crusades were over, the great trade routes were controlled by Christian merchants.

Very few Jews were farmers. Craftsmen and skilled laborers had formed societies called guilds. No Jew was permitted to enter a guild. As we saw, they were no longer traders. One occupation was still open to them—money-lending.

No Christian was supposed to charge another Christian interest. This rule was not strictly followed. Some Christians did act as money-lenders. Those Jews who had funds left from their mercantile days set up as money-lenders. The risks were great. Some money borrowed would never be repaid. Therefore the interest rate was high. Princes and nobles borrowed and found many a pretext for not repaying their debts. Church officials took large sums and then called the lenders "usurers," or men who charged too much interest. Peasants and soldiers borrowed and joined in a riot against the hated money-lenders. Even when times were fairly stable, the position of the Jews grew more difficult because of this occupation.

Nearly all the popes kept a watchful eye on the Jews. They refused to permit men and women who had been forcibly converted to return to their own faith. In 1215 one of the popes offered a resolution which was passed at a large church council. The order went forth that every Jew and Jewess was to wear a badge on his clothing. The yellow badge was the sign of lowliness. It set Jews apart—a separate people. But every Jew knew his brother and was ready to help him.

When a man held his family together and returned with them to their home, even if it was in ruins, he managed to pick up the thread of his life. One who had formerly been a rich merchant became a money-lender; a small trader opened a tiny store; a craftsman went from door to door, mending, repairing, tinkering. And always there was the rabbi to turn to for guidance.

What of those people who lost their families and whose communities were destroyed? Many of them became wanderers, begging their way from town to town. Jewish settlements, though they had troubles of their own, took care of them. An inn was set up for strangers and families opened their doors to them. Students found rabbis with whom they could continue studying.

Such was the general picture of the Jews in Europe. Now let us look at some individual countries and see how Jews fared in each one.

TALK OVER IN CLASS

What was the goal which the pope set for the Crusades? What were the aims of the Crusaders? How did the Crusades change the life of Jews in Central Europe? What was the final outcome of the Crusades—for Christians, for Moslems, for Jews?

What forced Jews to turn to money-lending as an occupation?

How did Jews fulfill the words, "Kol Yisroel Chaverim"—"All Jews Are Brothers," in time of trouble?

READ

The Heaven on the Sea by Ish-Kishor, "The Rabbi of Tortosa," p. 153.

28. FROM LAND TO LAND

ENGLAND IS a country which we have mentioned only in passing. When William the Conqueror came from Normandy in 1066 he brought Jews with him. For many years they held a favored position in his realm. The king was their direct overseer. He appointed a Chief Rabbi in charge of affairs. The Jews supplied the monarch with large sums of money in taxes and in loans. Some of them became wealthy and lived in fine homes. Abraham Ibn Ezra's patron was one of these men.

A number of Englishmen found Judaism attractive and satisfying and were converted. The Church was greatly offended and did its best to make life unpleasant. In 1218 English Jews were ordered to wear a white badge.

The Crusades affected Jews in England indirectly. King Richard, the Lion-Hearted, who had been their protector, left the country to lead the Third Crusade. After his departure, lies and rumors were spread about them. Harsh decrees were enacted against them.

Later rulers did not need Jewish assistance. They had taken such large sums from Jews that the great fortunes had disappeared. Great Christian Italian banking concerns, which had world-wide connections, took the place of Jewish bankers in England. A king who did not find Jews useful rarely protected them.

At last an order came for expulsion. In 1290, the 16,000 Jews of England were forced to leave. They crossed the Channel to Europe. For three hundred and fifty years no Jew was found in England.

In some parts of France the picture was a little brighter. The Jews were fortunate to have in their midst the pupils of Rashi. While Crusaders thundered past, these men continued to study as Rashi had taught. They were called the "Tosafists" or the ones who "add," because their writings were added to Rashi's commentaries. Jewish study could never stand still.

One of the most important of the Tosafists was Rabbi Tam, a grandson of Rashi. He was not only a great scholar; he was a rabbi who dealt with the problems of the day. Rabbi Tam lost nearly all he owned, except his books, in the Second Crusade. However, he kept on with his scholarly work.

Many problems had to be faced. Rabbi Tam called together one hundred and fifty rabbis from France and Germany to consider what was to be done to hold Jewish life together in an orderly fashion. Such a gathering was called a synod. Fifty years later another synod was held in Germany when the effects of the Crusades were more strongly felt. This meeting passed some important rulings. One of them was that taxes should be distributed fairly among rich and poor. The rabbis were determined that though a king might rule unjustly, Jews would regulate their own life righteously.

The kings of France took the Jews under their personal control. Each ruler treated them as the needs of the moment arose. Sometimes the king listened to evil-doers. One converted Jew, named Nicholas Donin, induced the king of France to put the Talmud on trial. The trial took place in Paris. Donin set out to prove that many statements in the Talmud spoke against Christianity. Rabbi Yechiel of Paris spoke for the Talmud. Facing the Queen Mother of France and a panel of hostile judges, what chance had he? The truth did not count. The Talmud was condemned.

Monks went from town to village seeking copies of the Talmud. Twenty-four cartloads were gathered and burnt in Paris in 1242. The reverent work of hundreds of scribes, the labor of years and years, was lost on that June day.

In 1306 the king decided to expel Jews from France. He thought he would profit best by taking over their property which they could not take along. They settled in nearby districts. Nine years later, the next king invited them to return. This monarch believed he could raise some more money from taxes. Only a few years later, after a period of great disorder, the Jews of France were sent out again. Twenty-five years later they were asked to return. Again the promises of French rulers were false. By 1394, the Jews had finally been expelled from nearly all of France.

These French Jews are credited with starting the practice of insuring their possessions when they had to send them to new homes, over land and sea. Such insurance is called Marine Insurance. Necessity drove the wanderers to find a way to protect their belongings—a way that is still widely used today—seven hundred years later.

Troubles came also to southern France. Jews were not the only sufferers. Their Christian neighbors had never joined the Church of Rome. They were more liberal in their ideas than most Christians of their time. They believed in the saying, "How good and how pleasant it is for brethren to dwell together in unity." The pope sent an army against them. These fine Christians were overcome and the Jewish settlements in southern France disappeared.

The Jews of Germany were in the saddest state of all. They looked for ways to better themselves. A group of them decided to emigrate from Germany. Their leader was Rabbi Meir of Rothenberg. Safely they journeyed to Italy. By chance, the rabbi was recognized. He was made a prisoner. The German emperor demanded a large ransom to free his prisoner. He declared that Rabbi Meir had no right to leave his land.

The Jews collected the money for the ransom. But Rabbi Meir refused to be freed. He would not set an example that could bring more trouble to Jews in other cities. For the emperor could fall on any group of Jews with claims for ransom.

Rabbi Meir stuck to his resolve. He remained in prison for many years. Fortunately, he was well treated and continued to be a religious leader even from there. He answered questions and continued with his learned writings. He died in prison—a captive by his own decision.

The brave story of Rabbi Meir was known in every home. It cheered men and women suffering under great burdens. For, some years later fresh troubles arose. A plague called the "Black Death" swept through Germany and France in 1348 and 1349. Thousands of people died from the plague. It was a contagious disease carried by rats and easily caught in the crowded and unsanitary conditions of medieval life. Doctors did not know the cause of the epidemic and could do little to help. The rumor spread that Jews had poisoned wells and were responsible for the plague. They had to flee from their homes. Many Jews died from the Black Death, but to their numbers must be added those who lost their lives at the hands of men who listened to the wicked rumors.

After the Black Death had run its course, Jews were permitted to return to some cities in Germany which needed whatever little money they still could squeeze from them. One of the conditions which was made was that they were to live together in a certain section of the town. Often the Jewish quarter was behind gates which were locked each night. This was the beginning of the ghetto in Germany.

Nearly every remainder of freedom was gone. The hardest work brought only a meager existence. The badge and the ghetto were the signs of the great decline in Jewish life.

In his home, however, the Jew found dignity. The poorest family observed the Sabbath and had a little treat for the day of rest. As soon as a community was reestablished the children were taught Torah. In the synagogue peace was found in prayer and study.

There was always at least one outstanding rabbi in the country who had authority, to whom the people listened. When it seemed that unworthy men were seeking to become rabbis, an edict went forth to the synagogues. Only a man who could bring a certificate from a well-known rabbi was to be called a rabbi. More than a thousand years earlier, at another time of danger, Rabbi Jochanan ben Zakkai ordained

his students by laying his hands on the head of each pupil when he was ready to be a teacher and rabbi. The ceremony of ordination was brought to life again. A rabbi had to be worthy of his high position. Jealously the Jews guarded the pillars of their inner life.

By the close of the fifteenth century, the Jews were moving to eastern Europe. During these days they could not create new works of science, poetry, or Jewish wisdom. Steadfastly

they held on to their religious beliefs, their hopes for God's blessing, and their determination to rear their children in the ways of their people. Most of the Jews in America today are the heirs of their firm faith and their piety.

TALK OVER IN CLASS

When books are burnt are they forgotten? What purpose do men have when they burn books? Do you think they accomplish their purpose?

A FIVE-MINUTE PLAY

The name of this play is "The Rabbi and the King." Your characters will be:

Rabbi Meir of Rothenberg
The Emperor of Germany
A Delegation of Jews

Base your play on the scene when the delegation of Jews comes to the emperor with the money to free the rabbi. Talk over what they would say, and Rabbi Meir's answer. How would the emperor act? This scene should make an interesting play.

DO YOU REMEMBER

What rabbi gave up his life to ordain his pupils?
How did this story come to be part of Jewish tradition?
Where was it written down? (A hint. Reread page 142.)

READ

Watchmen of the Night by Kalisher, "The Martyr of Germany," p. 71.

Unit 9

An End and a Beginning

Rarely do two eras of history come together so dramatically as they did in the year 1492. The end of one period saw the daring beginnings of another.

A group of people stood homeless on the shores of Spain. They watched as a small caravan of ships set out to conquer the vastness of the Atlantic. Did they realize how much they were a part of that great adventure? Did they know that some of their own people were sailing on those ships, and that others had equipped the enterprise with money and scientific knowledge?

They could not know that as they left one world behind them a new world was about to open to their descendants.

The past made way for the future.

August 2, 1492

29. THE LAST CENTER IN SPAIN

THE JEWS of Spain lived almost in a world apart. They were untouched by the Crusades. They were able to hold their heads high until about the end of the 1300's. When the badge was ordered in 1212, so many Spanish Jews made ready to leave the country that the king, Christian though he was, decided not to follow the pope's instructions. He asked them to remain. They did not wear the badge. In the next century, when the Black Death came to Spain, and the king of Castile was a victim of the plague, the hateful rumors of Jewish responsibility were never brought up.

Jews were well received at court. They continued to be the financial advisers to the monarch. Jewish scholars translated for one Spanish sovereign books on navigation and astronomy and works on precious stones. He also asked to have some parts of the Talmud translated into Spanish for his benefit.

Wealthy Jews sometimes stirred up anger against themselves because of their fine clothes, elegant carriages, and splendid homes. Christians were envious of such display and modest Jews felt it was not wise.

For the most part, middle class and poorer Jews were engaged in industry and agriculture. They employed Christians in their homes and had business ventures together with Christians.

Jewish communities regulated their own affairs with the rabbi in charge, and judges chosen from amongst themselves. Taxes were collected for the king, charity was given to those in need, and schools for young pupils and Talmudic students were found all over.

This was the picture of confidence and security which Spanish Jewish life presented on the surface during the thirteenth and fourteenth centuries. Below there were warnings, like the rumblings of thunder which are heard when a storm is near.

At first the warnings were mild. The enemies of the Jews proceeded carefully. Jews were not killed or injured. The method was to break down the high position of Jews in the country.

The most active foes were a group of monks called the Dominican Friars. They began by urging the king to take privileges away from the Jews. Then they called on the Jews to defend their religion before the world.

Among the Dominicans was a converted Jew named Pablo Christiani. He suggested that a public debate, called a disputation, take place between him and a rabbi to discuss certain parts of the Talmud.

The outstanding rabbi of Spain was Rabbi Moses ben Nachman, or Nachmanides. Sometimes he is called RaMBaN, from the initials of his name. He lived from 1195 to 1270.

The picture we have of Nachmanides is that of a fine, warm-hearted person and a great Talmudic scholar. His learning taught him faith. He followed the teachings of earlier scholars, rather than write boldly of new ideas, like Maimonides. Moses ben Nachman is often considered the representative of those whose ideal was faith and tradition. Moses ben Maimon was the leader of those men who judged ideas and teachings with the mind, in the light of reason. Nevertheless, both men held the same religious ideas; the belief in God and His goodness, the coming of the Messiah and the holiness of the Torah.

Ramban had to accept the challenge of the disputation. It took place in the palace of the king in Barcelona in 1263.

Pablo Christiani based his arguments on the agaddic portions of the Talmud. Nachmanides explained that the Agaddah contained fanciful explanations which did not have to be accepted. He pointed out that the Halacha was the code of Jewish law.

One of the main questions that was discussed was whether or not the Messiah had come; that is, was Jesus the Messiah. Nachmanides made one telling point after another. He was seventy years old at the time and he conducted himself with great dignity. The king and his courtiers were impressed. Nachmanides was not overawed at the presence of his sovereign. He declared that the Messiah was supposed to bring in an era of peace. However, he continued, Christians were waging war in many places. Fearlessly he faced the king and said, "If the Messianic era is at hand, O Sire, then it is time for thee and thy knights to put an end to war."

The disputation continued for four days. Nachmanides clearly vanquished his opponent. The king spoke to him privately and gave him a gift of gold.

The Dominicans were greatly dissatisfied. They were strong enough to receive permission to send Pablo Christiani from synagogue to synagogue to preach to unwilling Jews.

Nachmanides published the statements he had made. The Dominicans made this an excuse to urge the king to exile Nachmanides. Against his will, the monarch gave in to their demand.

Nachmanides was sent away from his native land. He went to Palestine. The Jews there received him with open arms. Jerusalem had just been the scene of many battles and was in ruins. Through Nachmanides' influence, a synagogue was built and a school was opened. He taught in the Holy Land until his death. Perhaps in the end he felt that exile was worth while, for it enabled him to fulfill the wish of the pious Jew of his day—to spend his last days in Erets Yisroel, and to be buried there.

After Nachmanides, many other fine rabbis and teachers became known. Spain was still the place for Jewish study. In Barcelona an excellent school was set up. The head of the school, Rabbi Solomon Ibn Adret, was a great Talmudic authority. While Jewish life was breaking up in so many places, Spain was still firm and stable. Ibn Adret was consulted on all sorts of problems. He wrote thousands of responsa. Ibn Adret counseled strict observance of the laws of the Talmud.

Many rabbis fled from their homes in France and Germany. One rabbi who was forced to leave Germany came to Toledo and established a fine school. The students devoted themselves almost entirely to the Talmud. The rabbis frowned on the study of science. How different from the days of the Golden Age!

One thoughtful student of the Law prepared an important book along the lines of the *Yad Hachazakah* by Maimonides. It was also a code of laws carefully arranged, with the opinions for and against each of them, which different rabbis had made since the days of the Talmud. It was shorter than the "Yad" and left out laws which were no longer in use, like the laws of the Temple. This book had an interesting name. It was called *Turim* or "Rows" and referred to the rows of jewels worn by the High Priest of the Temple on his breastplate. For almost two hundred years the *Turim* was followed closely by rabbis to help them regulate Jewish life according to Jewish law.

Just at the time when science was losing its hold on Jewish students and when study was confined almost entirely to the Talmud and books by Jewish scholars, a new system of ideas began to receive a great deal of attention. This system was called the Kabala and explained the Torah and history in mysterious ways.

The Kabalists centered their thoughts and their writing on God. They tried to understand His relation to man. Their question was: How can a man come close to God? Many of them were not content to pray in the usual manner. They added chants and unusual ceremonies to long hours of prayer. A follower of the Kabala often sat lost in thoughts of another world where God reigned.

The Kabalists examined the Bible differently than it had

been examined before. They believed that each word in the Bible had more than one meaning—a simple, ordinary meaning and a hidden meaning. Numbers had hidden meanings. The letters of the Hebrew alphabet had always been used for counting—Aleph stood for 1, Beis for 2, and so on through the entire alphabet. The Kabalists combined letters and numbers in a new way.

Here is an example of how letters and numbers were interchanged by Kabalists to find hidden meanings. The letters of the word "tov," which means good, add up to 17, so the number 17 stood for the idea of goodness, or simply good. The two letters in the word "chai," which means life, add up to 18. In our own day, people contribute "chai" dollars to charity. It gives them a good feeling to connect a fine deed with the idea of life. How surprised these people would be if they were told they are following in the footsteps of the Kabalists!

The Kabalists also believed that they could foretell events like the coming of the Messiah, by counting the numerical value of certain phrases in the Bible.

At first the Kabala was studied orally. Its teachings were handed down by word of mouth secretly from teacher to pupil. Then books for study were written. The most impor-

tant book was called the "Zohar" or "Brightness." The Zohar explains the hidden meanings which Kabalists found in the Bible. It was prepared by Moses de Leon. However, he said it was written many years earlier by Rabbi Simon ben Yochai who lived in the days of Judah ha-Nasi. It is easy to prove that Rabbi Simon could not have written the Zohar, for in it are references to events which happened after he died. Moses knew that Rabbi Simon's name would give the Zohar great importance. He followed an old custom. You remember that some books of the Bible carry King Solomon's name, although he did not write them.

Most thoughtful students of the Law did not accept the Kabala. Its strange ideas could only lead people astray. But it influenced Jews and some Christians for years to come. As a matter of fact, some excellent Talmudists had leanings toward the Kabala. Nachmanides permitted some of its ideas to influence his writings.

The Kabala had many followers all over Europe. You can see how men could lose themselves in curious calculations and strange guesses as an escape from the troubles of real life. It led them nowhere, but it brought them comfort in times which grew harder day by day.

QUESTIONS TO ANSWER

What do we call a disputation today?
What were the first signs of unrest in Spain?
How did life in Christian Spain compare with life in France, Germany, and England in the thirteenth and fourteenth centuries?
What system of religious thinking became popular?
What was the name of the book which told about it?
Who was supposed to be its author?

READINGS FOR TEACHERS

Unit 9 (*CHAPTERS 29–30*)

A History of the Jewish People by Margolis and Marx, Chaps. LI-LIV, LVI, LVIII-LXIII.

A History of the Jews, Book III, by Grayzel, Chaps. IV-VIII.

The Jew in the Medieval World by Marcus, "Innocent and the Jews," p. 137; "Rashi's Grandson and the Crusades," p. 304.

30. AFTER FIVE HUNDRED YEARS

THE DAYS of peaceful study and happy security came to an abrupt end. The warnings reached a climax. The storm broke. It followed after a civil war and quarrels among the ruling family. Jews at the court were in and then out of favor. The time of turmoil and disorder was seized on for the attack. One of the first signs was the badge. In 1371 Jews were compelled to wear the yellow badges in Castile.

Twenty years later, the Jews of Seville were set upon by a mob of Christians who had been listening to an influential monk. He was the Queen Mother's own private priest. His words aroused the people to great violence. Some attempts were made by the king to check the riots but he was just a boy, and his efforts were too feeble to be of much help. The Juderia, or Jewish quarter of Seville, was burned, and its inhabitants driven out.

Toledo and Barcelona with their fine synagogues came next. The governor of Barcelona opened the doors of his fortress to the Jews. They fought valiantly for their families and their homes. Many died in battle.

The fighting, riots, and disorder lasted for about three months. In that short time a tremendous change took place.

Homes were gone and families were broken up. One basic change had come about. Thousands of Spanish Jews were baptized, far more than had been converted in France and in Germany. They became the New Christians, or Marranos, a Spanish word of ridicule, meaning "swine." A kinder Hebrew name for them is the "Anusim" or forced converts.

The New Christians were divided into two groups. The first were those men and women who readily took the opportunity to become Christians. Some of them had thought about it before. Judaism hampered them and held them back either in business or in social life.

The second group repented of their act. If they could, they would have returned to Judaism. This was impossible. The Church strictly forbade it. Some left the country for lands where they could once more be Jews. Others tried to be Jews in their homes and Christians to the world outside. They remembered fast days and holidays. As you will see, their hidden loyalty brought disaster both to them and to those who remained steadfast Jews.

Some baptized Jews were real trouble makers. A hundred years after a converted Jew challenged Nachmanides to a disputation, another converted Jew repeated the same type of challenge. Once more the Talmud was put on trial.

A disputation was called in the city of Tortosa. It lasted a year and nine months, during 1412 and 1413. Twenty-two rabbis were forced to attend sixty-eight meetings during this period to defend the Talmud against the untruths of a converted Jew. The result could have been foretold. Jews were forbidden to teach or to study the Talmud, and copies of the Talmud were taken from Jewish communities. Of course, such laws did not mean that Jews actually stopped studying the Talmud.

The organizers of the disputation were dissatisfied. Their most important aim had not been realized. They had hoped to convert at least some of the rabbis who took part in the dispute. Not even one of them was baptized. All went home firmer than ever in their faith.

At almost the very time that these staunch men were defending their beliefs, thousands of Jews were forced to listen to a Dominican friar, who traveled from city to city. He carried a Torah in his hands and came to Jews assembled in their synagogues. With him came an angry mob. The results were thousands of conversions.

Seventy-five strange years passed. From day to day, no one knew what would happen. Any city could be the scene of an attack. On the other hand, Jews continued to hold important positions. Rarely was there a king without a Jewish tax-collector or financial adviser. Most royal families and important courtiers used only Jewish physicians. These men were often

able to influence the monarchs to take back a law or to soften a harsh decree. There was always the chance that things would change for the better.

The time came when the pleas of ministers were of no avail. A greedy king and a narrow-minded queen united with the pope and his officials to stamp out "heresy," or what they considered false religious ideas.

The false religious idea, of course, was Judaism. The eyes of the Church were directed to the New Christians. Many of them had grown careless and in numerous ways showed that their Christianity was but a mask. They observed the Sabbath as best they could by wearing clean clothes and placing a cloth on their dinner table. A man might bless his children and omit the sign of the cross. On Yom Kippur, he could not enter the synagogue, but he could go barefoot. In such small ways, the New Christians showed their allegiance to Judaism. Some of them received instruction secretly from Jews.

The New Christians were everywhere. No bars were placed against them in business or in the professions. Some were priests and bishops. Churchmen encouraged them to marry into important Christian families to hold them to their new faith. Old Christians hated them and were jealous of their success.

The two greatest kingdoms in Spain were united when Isabella of Castile married Ferdinand of Aragon. The queen had made a vow to rid her land of unbelievers. She gave the church officials the right to use a cruel instrument, the Inquisition.

The Inquisition was a religious court. The men and women who were brought before it were charged with heresy. Long imprisonment in horrid dungeons and torture were used to force them to confess.

The judges were not satisfied with confession. As the price of mercy, they demanded the names of others who were guilty of disbelief. A chain of names, extending from one end of Spain to the other, was obtained.

Mercy was promised but rarely granted. The end for thousands of New Christians was death at the stake. Their property was divided between the king and the church—an arrangement which was satisfying to both.

A simple question was asked. What about the chief unbelievers, the Jews? Were they to remain untouched? For, in spite of all the conversions, the great majority of the Jews were steadfast. Neither the hope of reward nor the threat of death had moved them. Ferdinand, Isabella, and the Church realized at last that they would never succeed in converting all the Jews. They came to a cruel decision. Every Jew was ordered to leave Spain within four months.

It is hard to believe, but the king and queen saw nothing strange in the fact that the man who had been their chief financial adviser for years was a Jew, Isaac Abrabanel. Abrabanel went with a companion to the palace. He offered the royal couple an enormous sum of gold to recall the cruel decree. Ferdinand was on the brink of accepting, when the head

of the Inquisition made a dramatic entrance, carrying a cross in his hand. Abrabanel's plea was lost.

More than 150,000 Jews were exiled from Spain. For some it had been their fathers' home for nearly 1,500 years. For all of them, it was the land they loved, bound up with proud memories.

At the end, every Jew helped his brother. The rich shared with the poor, so each had something to help him on his way when he departed.

Most of the exiles left from two points, Seville and Toledo. From Seville, they went to North Africa, to Italy, to Egypt, and to Palestine. Many went to Turkey, where they were well received, and in time made a fine home in that land.

Those who assembled in Toledo crossed the border to Portugal. They received a warm welcome, but it did not last long. The arm of the Inquisition reached into Portugal, when its king married a Spanish princess. At first the Jews were given permission to leave. But the king hated to lose so many fine citizens. The right to depart was taken back. Some Jews stole away. The rest were forcibly converted. In less than a hundred years, not a single Jew remained on the entire peninsula of Spain.

The story of Spanish Jewry was not wiped out by exile. Its poetry lived wherever Jews gathered. The wisdom of its scientists was carried over land and sea. The teachings of its sages about the Bible and the Talmud were studied in schools in far-off cities. Its own special synagogue ritual was transplanted to new homes where it lives today.

According to the Hebrew calendar, August 2, 1492, when the last Jews left Spain, was the 9th of Ov. You know that this is the anniversary of the destruction of the First and the Second Temples.

Another event happened that day. As Jews set sail for unknown destinations, three small ships also left the harbor and sailed past them. The ships were the "Nina," the "Pinta," and the "Santa Maria."

Columbus set out to discover a new land. Much of the money for his expedition came from New Christians. Some of his companions were descended from Jewish families. Some of the maps which guided him were the work of a Jewish mapmaker. How fitting that Jews should have had a goodly share in the discovery of the land where the light of freedom was to shine for them and for all who sought liberty!

Yet the New World was not the only place where Jewish genius was to be given an opportunity. Many more fine chapters of history would be written in the Old Worlds of Europe, Africa, and Asia.

TALK OVER IN CLASS

Jews were being persecuted in Spain at the same time that some of them were advisers to the king.

Marranos were officials of the church while practicing Judaism secretly.

The last day Jews spent on Spanish soil was the day Columbus set sail to discover America.

Make up a title for each of these statements.

READ

In Many Lands by Elma E. Levinger, "The Man Who Came Late," p. 13.

The Bar Mitzvah Treasury edited by Eisenberg, "Bar Mitzvah in Spain" by A. A. Kabak, p. 260.

Great Men in Israel by Weis, "With a Song on Their Lips," p. 110; "How Columbus Discovered America," p. 115.

Watchmen of the Night by Kalisher, "Adviser to the King," p. 79.

The Great March, Book II, by Lurie, "Whither Now?" p. 217.

CHILDREN'S READING LIST

BELTH, NORMAN (ed.), *The World-Over Story Book,* Bloch Publishing Co.

BURSTEIN, ABRAHAM, *Judah Halevi in Granada,* Bloch Publishing Co.

———, *The Boy of Cordova,* Bloch Publishing Co.

———, *The Boy Called Rashi,* Behrman House, Inc.

COMINS, HARRY L. and REUBEN LEAF, *Arts-Crafts for the Jewish Club,* Union of American Hebrew Congregations.

EISENBERG, AZRIEL (ed.), *The Bar Mitzvah Treasury,* Behrman House, Inc.

GAER, JOSEPH, *The Unconquered,* Union of American Hebrew Congregations.

GAMORAN, MAMIE G., *Days and Ways,* Union of American Hebrew Congregations.

ISH-KISHOR, SULAMITH, *The Heaven on the Sea,* Bloch Publishing Co.

KALISHER, BETTY, *Watchmen of the Night,* Union of American Hebrew Congregations.

LEVINGER, ELMA EHRLICH, *Great Jewish Women,* Behrman House, Inc.

———, *Great Jews Since Bible Times,* Behrman House, Inc.

———, *In Many Lands,* Bloch Publishing Co.

LURIE, ROSE G., *The Great March, Book II,* Union of American Hebrew Congregations.

MILLGRAM, ABRAHAM E., *The Sabbath Book,* Jewish Publication Society.

MYERS, JACK M., *The Story of the Jewish People,* Vols. I and II, Bloch Publishing Co.

Pilchik, Ely M., *Hillel*, Henry Schuman, Inc.
Posy, Arnold, *Israeli Tales and Legends*, Bloch Publishing Co.
Union Hymnal, The, Central Conference of American Rabbis.
Union Prayerbook I, The, Newly Revised, Central Conference of American Rabbis.
Weis, J. Max, *Great Men in Israel*, Bloch Publishing Co.
Zeligs, Dorothy F., *A Child's History of Jewish Life*, Bloch Publishing Co.

TEACHER'S BIBLIOGRAPHY

BILDERSEE, ADELE, *Jewish Post-Biblical History,* Union of American Hebrew Congregations.

CAPLAN, SAMUEL and HAROLD U. RIBALOV, *The Great Jewish Books,* Horizon Press, Inc.

EISENBERG, AZRIEL (ed.), *The Bar Mitzvah Treasury,* Behrman House, Inc.

FEUER, LEON I. and AZRIEL EISENBERG, *Jewish Literature Since the Bible, Book I,* Union of American Hebrew Congregations.

FREEHOF, SOLOMON B., *The Responsa Literature,* Jewish Publication Society.

GRAYZEL, SOLOMON, *A History of the Jews,* Jewish Publication Society.

KOBLER, FRANZ (ed.), *A Treasury of Jewish Letters,* East and West Library.

MARCUS, JACOB RADER, *The Jew in the Medieval World,* Union of American Hebrew Congregations.

MARGOLIS, MAX L. and ALEXANDER MARX, *A History of the Jewish People,* Jewish Publication Society.

MYERS, JACK M., *The Story of the Jewish People,* Bloch Publishing Co.

PILCHIK, ELY M., *Hillel,* Henry Schuman, Inc.

SCHAUSS, HAYYIM, *The Jewish Festivals,* Union of American Hebrew Congregations.

SCHECHTER, SOLOMON, *Studies in Judaism,* 2nd Series, Jewish Publication Society.

VOGELSTEIN, HERMANN, *History of the Jews in Rome,* Jewish Publication Society.

BIBLIOGRAPHY FOR ARTS-CRAFTS AND ACTIVITIES

COMINS, HARRY L. and REUBEN LEAF, *Arts-Crafts for the Jewish Club,* Union of American Hebrew Congregations.

GRAND, SAMUEL (ed.), *Audio-Visual Education in the Jewish Religious School,* Union of American Hebrew Congregations.

PESSIN, DEBORAH and TEMIMA GEZARI, *The Jewish Kindergarten,* Union of American Hebrew Congregations.

SHAFTEL, GEORGE and FANNIE R., *Role Playing,* National Conference of Christians and Jews.

Pronouncing List

Key to Pronunciation

ā—pay, ă—bad, ä—art, ȧ—Adȧ; ē—me, ĕ—bed, ẽ—her; ī—ice, ĭ—thin; ō—go, ŏ—odd, ô—orb; ū—rule, ŭ—run, û—unite.

Aaron ben Meir—Ā'-rŏn bĕn Mā'-ēr
Abrabanel—Ă-brā'-bă-nĕl
Adiabene—Ă-dĭ-ă-bē'-nē
Almohades—Ăl-mō-hā'-dēs
Amoraim—Ă-mō-rä'-yĭm
Antipater—Ăn-tĭp'-ă-tẽr
Aristobulus—Ă-rĭs-tŏb'-û-lŭs
Bethar—Bĕ-tär'
Bulan—Bû'-lăn
Caesarea—Sē-sä-rē'-ȧ
Caliph—Kā'-lĭf
Chanoch—Chä-nōch'
Charlemagne—Shär'-lĕ-mān
Exilarch—Ĕx'-ĭ-lärk
Gamaliel—Gä-mä'-lē-ĕl
Gaon—Gā'-ŏn
Geniza—Gĕ-nē'-zȧ
Geonim—Gĕ-ō'-nĭm
Giora—Gē-ō'-rȧ
Hyrcanus—Hŭr'-că-nŭs
Idumeans—Ī-dū-mē'-ăns
Islam—Ĭs-läm'
Izates—Ĭ-zä'-tēs
Kabala—Kä-bä'-lä
Kallah—Kä'-lä
Khazars—Kä-zärs'
Kuzari—Kū'-ză-rē
Maimonides—Mī-mŏn'-ĭ-dēs
Mariamne—Mă-rē-ăm'-nē
Marranos—Mă-rä'-nōs
Mayence—Mīnts
Moreh N'vuchim—Mō-rĕ' N'vū'-chēm
Nachmanides—Näch-män'-ĭ-dēs
Nehardea—Nĕ-här-dē'-ȧ
Pirkei Ovos—Pĭr-kā' Ō-vōs'
Pompey—Pŏm-pā'
Ravina—Ră-vē'-nȧ
Saadiah Gaon—Să-äd'-yă Gā'-ŏn
Salome—Să'-lō-māy
Sepphoris—Sĕ-fō'-rĭs
Septuagint—Sĕp-tū'-ă-jĭnt
Sholosh R'golim—Shô-lōsh' R'gô-lĭm'
Tannaim—Tä-nī'-yĭm
Vespasian—Vĕs-pā'-sĭ-ăn
Yad Hachazakah—Yäd Hä-chä-zä'-kä

INDEX